LINDSAY KEMENY

THE SCIENCE OF READING IN PRACTICE

ROCK YOUR LITERACY BLOCK

Mighty Moves to Organize Your Day and Optimize Student Learning

SCHOLASTIC

**To Aubrey,
for cheering me on
every time I write**

Senior Vice President and Publisher: Tara Welty
Editorial Director: Sarah Longhi
Editor-in-Chief: Raymond Coutu
Production Editor: Danny Miller
Assistant Editor: Samantha Unger
Cover design: Tannaz Fassihi
Interior design: Maria Lilja

ISBN 978-1-5461-8800-1

2 3 4 5 6 7 8 9 10 40 34 33 32 31 30 29 28 27 26

Scholastic Inc., 557 Broadway, New York, NY 10012

CONTENTS

ACKNOWLEDGMENTS

I couldn't do what I do without the support of my incredible husband. Thank you, Steve, for everything you do to support me and our kids. You pick up the pieces and so much more. I'm also grateful for the unwavering support of my four children. Thank you for your encouragement and patience as I write, speak, and teach. I love you all!

It's an extraordinary honor to have Louisa Moats, a pioneer in the field, contribute the foreword to my book. Her generous words and positivity are gifts I'll always cherish.

Words cannot express how grateful I am to Pam Kastner for reviewing each draft chapter. She is a guiding light to so many educators and I'm thankful she has shared her brilliance with me. I'm also deeply appreciative to Leslie Laud for not only reviewing a draft chapter, but also for coaching me in effective writing instruction. Her guidance has been invaluable.

I feel so lucky to have such a wonderful team at Scholastic. Thanks to Ray Coutu, Sarah Longhi, Tara Welty, Danny Miller, Tannaz Fassihi, Maria Lilja, Samantha Unger, and many others. I'm grateful for how they spark ideas, refine my writing, and have created a visually stunning book. I'm also thankful for the marketing team, including Danielle Donnelly and Jacqueline Biltucci and all the amazing AEs for their support and assistance in spreading my message.

It means the world to me to have the support of so many educators. Putting a book out into the world can be daunting, so each kind comment, message, and review is sincerely appreciated. Your encouragement keeps me going and helps me have the courage to continue to share.

Finally, I am thankful to all the teachers who give their all day after day. Not only do you work tirelessly for your students, here you are reading a book about teaching in your spare time! Thank you for your dedication. I love teaching and am proud to be among you. We have the power to be a beacon of hope for the students we work with. What a gift!

FOREWORD
by Louisa Cook Moats

Lindsay Kemeny's first book, *7 Mighty Moves*, is a down-to-earth guide to research-backed and classroom-tested reading instruction, written by a knowledgeable and effective first-grade teacher. In this sequel, Lindsay shares much, much more about how, exactly, she moves 20+ children through a literacy block to maximize learning of content and skills.

Skilled teachers constantly make decisions that improve classroom atmosphere and flow. This book gives the reader valuable insight into exactly what those decisions entail. Lindsay identifies dozens of practical instructional and classroom-management strategies that ensure student engagement and retention of learning, smooth transitions, and a positive climate, and addresses all the critical aspects of literacy instruction. With clear directives and supporting rationales, she offers "do's" and "don'ts" and "good, better, best" summaries of what works for each component of the literacy block, beginning from the moment children walk through the classroom door.

In this tidy, "no frills" book, Lindsay tackles every relevant topic. Her wisdom and understanding of research-based practice are reflected in the attention she devotes not only to teaching foundational reading skills, but also to building language comprehension, which in turn fosters a love of reading. Loving to read is fostered very early as a consequence of knowing both *how* to read and sharing with other people the *joy* of learning about others' minds, hearts, experiences, and ways of life. To that end, Lindsay shows how to select provocative and beautifully written texts and how to read them aloud so that students become engrossed. She also includes tips on locating literature that will captivate children from the first page.

Much of the guidance in this book is grounded squarely in reading research. Lindsay continues to be a student of reading science and has been quick to learn and adapt key research findings into her teaching practice. She incorporates newer best practices, such as writing strategies adapted from *thinkSRSD* (Laud & Patel, 2023), and her advice on building phoneme awareness skills aligns squarely with best evidence at this point. As she points out, phoneme awareness should be integrated into a code-based lesson, and phoneme identification should be supported with reference to articulation. Furthermore, Lindsay's advice about sound-spelling walls is right on: Get to the phoneme level of word analysis quickly and spend only a few minutes per day building phoneme awareness, as a precursor to a phonics and/or spelling lesson. Only use a "sound wall" if the purpose of it is clear to you and your students—as a bridge to the phonics lesson.

Where research is unclear or nonexistent, Lindsay is unafraid to take a position and defend it based on common sense and experience. For example, early in the book, she states that a 90-minute literacy block, especially in first grade, is insufficient to accomplish all the instruction that is necessary for desired results. I couldn't agree more. In our five-year Early Interventions Project, carried out in Washington, DC, public schools, Barbara Foorman and I identified the need for a literacy block of two or more hours until students have acquired foundational skills, based on our observational data (2008).

On that theme, Lindsay's accounting of what to do and for how long to do it conveys her acute awareness of the value of every minute of a school day. School may be the only place where children can hear academic vocabulary, listen to well-written literature, answer questions on their understanding of text, or write about what they are learning. Time is precious, and Lindsay's classroom-management techniques ensure that students are rarely off task.

Rock Your Literacy Block is an excellent book, unique among the many about teaching reading. Lindsay Kemeny, a highly effective and motivated teacher, brings us into her mind, as well as her classroom, to reveal how, exactly, to implement effective literacy instruction. Thankfully, she avoids "fluff" and clearly communicates a detailed plan of action so that you, too, can "rock your literacy block."

—LOUISA COOK MOATS, Ed.D., Author of *LETRS Professional Development* and *Speech to Print: Language Essentials for Teachers*

Setting the Stage

INTRODUCTION

Having a son with dyslexia and depression completely changed the way I teach. His diagnosis sent me on a quest to discover not only what it would take to help him read proficiently, but also what it would take to help *all* students read proficiently. I was once so uncertain about how to help readers. Now my vision is clear.

I've also come to understand the tight connection between one's ability to read and one's self-esteem. After experiencing my son's harrowing words and actions, it was beautiful to see his heart heal and his confidence grow as his reading skills grew. My family and I did everything we could to alleviate his depression, especially as he was hitting rock bottom. What helped him the most, though, was strengthening his ability to read. As his reading improved, so did his self-esteem.

We can read studies and listen to experts to learn about evidence-based practices, but implementing what we're learning takes things to a whole other level. Sharing something you've learned about is different from sharing something you're actually *doing*. In this book, I share the things I'm doing. I am a classroom teacher, constantly figuring out how to

SPOTLIGHT ON THE SCIENCE OF READING

Sometimes, educators think the science of reading refers to a specific curriculum, program, or method. But the term actually refers to a large body of high-quality research on reading. It encompasses thousands of studies. Or, as literacy expert Louisa Moats puts it, "'The science of reading' is not an ideology, a philosophy, a political agenda, a one-size-fits-all approach, a program of instruction, or a specific component of instruction. It is the emerging consensus from many related disciplines, based on literally thousands of studies, supported by hundreds of millions of research dollars, conducted across the world in many languages" (Moats & Tolman, 2024).

I am grateful for the science of reading–so thankful for the many researchers, scholars, specialists, and literacy experts who have been sharing their knowledge and work for decades—for it healed my son's heart. I would not be the teacher I am today without the science of reading and those who inform it.

The Reading League offers an excellent free resource for understanding the science of reading entitled "Science of Reading: Defining Guide." Download it at the organization's website (thereadingleague.org).

best apply the research I learn about. Every year I adjust and refine how I do things. I'm not perfect, but I'm always working to improve and enhance my practice. I'm also committed to sharing what's working for me and my students, even if it's intimidating or nerve-racking, in the hope that I inspire you to become the best teacher you can be.

My Back Story

When my principal told me that she needed me to move from teaching second grade to first grade, I panicked and questioned whether I had what it took to make the shift. What are first graders like? How should I schedule the day and what should my literacy block look like? The first thing I did was reach out to first-grade teachers I admire in my school district. I then visited their classrooms and had them walk me through their literacy block. And let me tell you, that was the best decision. It was so helpful to listen in as they described their day and pulled back the curtain on their organization and planning. After those visits, I pondered the things they told me and couldn't get over the fact that I had never done this before. Listening to how others structure their day is so valuable!

So in this book, I aim to do exactly that: Walk you through my literacy block and show you how I organize it. I will not only share what my instruction looks like, but also transition tips and the behind-the-scenes glimpses of what I do and think about. Your literacy block does not need to look exactly like mine, but I hope, by sharing my approach, you gain insights and inspiration for designing your own block.

Who This Book Is for

What sets this book apart from so many others is that I speak from experience. To ensure the most accurate, practical, and targeted advice, I focus on kindergarten through second grade because I have taught those grades. While I've worked as an interventionist in grades three and higher, I haven't had the experience of designing a literacy block tailored to those grades, and, of course, intermediate teachers have their own needs that I don't have first-hand experience addressing. That said, if you teach older students, I'm confident you'll find many of the ideas in this book useful, but you'll likely need to adapt them.

What This Book Contains and How It's Organized

Rock Your Literacy Block focuses on how I structure my day and week, and what my literacy instruction looks like. Chapter 1 offers an overview of my block, with models of reading that inform my work as well as sample schedules and time allotments for each component of my block. It also shares ways to maximize the impact of your instruction because *how* we use those minutes is critical. From there, I walk you through the components, devoting a chapter to each one—from our morning arrival to our afternoon read-aloud.

Each chapter follows a predictable, seamless structure.

1. **"Spotlight":** a brief, birds-eye-view description of the component, with dominant moves from my book *7 Mighty Moves: Research-Backed, Classroom-Tested Strategies to Ensure K-to-3 Reading Success.*
2. **"Closer Look":** a more in-depth look at the component, specifically my instruction, routines, transitions, and thinking behind the component.
3. **"Schedule Considerations":** approximate time allocations for each part of the component and how they might vary from day to day, across the week, and throughout the year.
4. **"In Closing, Remember...":** a summary of important points.

There isn't one perfect way to structure your literacy block. The decisions we make exist on a continuum, from good to best. So, at the end of each chapter, I share ideas that will elevate your teaching from good to better to best.

And now I invite you into my classroom. Come on in and take a peek!

—Lindsay

Creating a Literacy Block That Truly ROCKS

CHAPTER 1

Understanding the pieces, or components, of literacy instruction is just part of the puzzle. Equally challenging is understanding how those pieces fit together to create a comprehensive framework—or "the literacy block." "What does your literacy block look like?" "Can you walk me through it?" "How many minutes do you spend on each part?" Those are common questions that teachers ask, and I always enjoy exploring answers. It's enlightening to see how different teachers structure their blocks. This sparks new ideas and prompts me to evaluate my own practices critically.

So just how much time should we allot for the literacy block? It seems the answer to that question is based on a combination of expert opinion and practical experience, mixed with research findings.

So just how much time should we allot for the literacy block? It seems the answer to that question is based on a combination of expert opinion and practical experience, mixed with research findings. A common recommendation is 90 minutes, and while there's a strong rationale for it, more research is needed to determine its effectiveness (Underwood, 2018). I'm going to come right out and say that I don't think you'll see

strong enough literacy gains for your K–2 students if you devote only 90 minutes to your literacy block. I'm baffled when I hear this recommendation and wonder what other activities are taking up so much instructional time. Recognized reading expert, Tim Shanahan, recommends devoting 120–180 minutes per day to reading and writing instruction (2019) and that recommendation resonates with me. My literacy block is typically 150 minutes a day. I discuss my schedule later in this chapter.

A Note on Students Who Need Extra Support

The literacy instruction described in this book is based on Tier 1 core instruction, or instruction for all students in your class. Students who need extra support should receive targeted intervention in addition to Tier 1 instruction. For example, if your core instruction is 150 minutes a day, students who need intervention would benefit from an additional 30 minutes, bringing their total instructional time to 180 minutes.

Models That Inform My Reading Instruction

I refer to two models of reading when I think about organizing my block.

The Simple View of Reading (Gough & Tunmer, 1986) helps me see the big picture. It makes it clear that reading comprehension is a result of word recognition *and* language comprehension. Students need instruction in both areas to become proficient readers. So I divide my daily instructional time between them. Moats and Tolman recommend that half of the ELA block in K and 1 be devoted to foundational skills and the other half to language comprehension. They go on to explain that the time devoted to building comprehension should increase as students progress in their foundational skills, usually in second and third grade (2024).

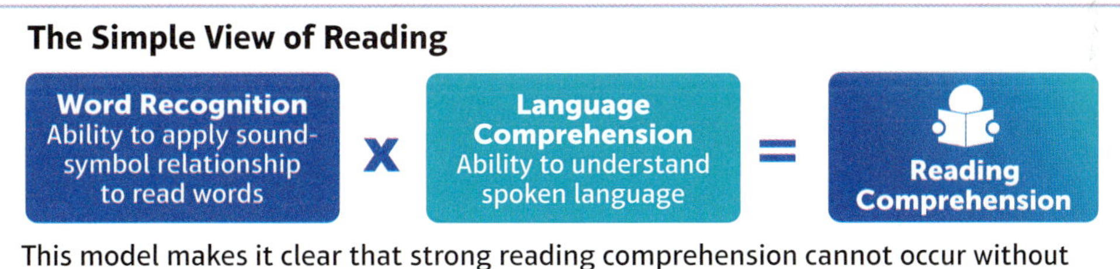

(Gough & Tunmer, 1986)

To go deeper, I lean on the Reading Rope (Scarborough, 2001). The bottom strands of the rope (phonological awareness, decoding, sight recognition) align with "word recognition," and the upper strands (background knowledge, vocabulary, language structures, verbal reasoning, literacy knowledge) align with "language comprehension."

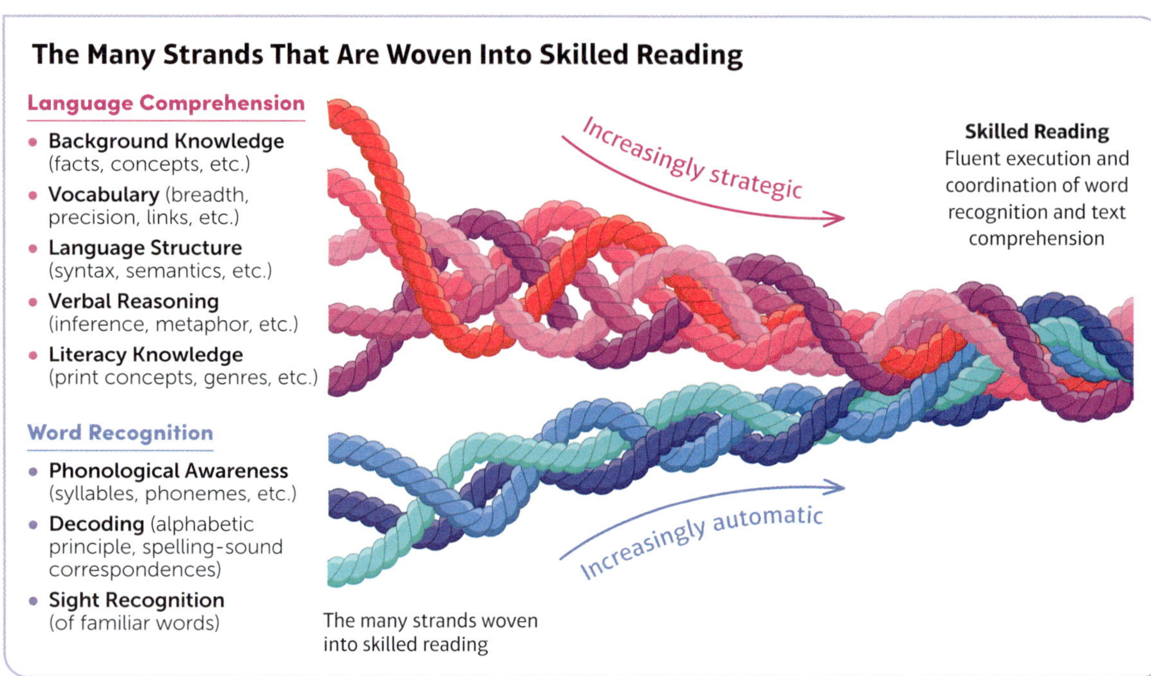

(Scarborough, 2001)

Both of those models provide a comprehensive view of reading. They, along with the Report of the National Reading Panel (2000) identifying five key components of reading: phonemic awareness, phonics, fluency, vocabulary, and comprehension, ensure I address all aspects of reading in my instruction.

A Closer Look at How I Divide My Time

Let's take a closer look at how much time I spend on the two areas of the Simple View: word recognition and language comprehension.

- I dedicate about 30–45 minutes daily to phonemic awareness and phonics, essential building blocks for developing strong word recognition.
- I spend 30 minutes giving a close-reading lesson, focusing on language comprehension—specifically, developing vocabulary and background knowledge, and teaching comprehension strategies.

Word Recognition	x	Language Comprehension	=	Reading Comprehension
Phonics Lesson (Fluency included): 30–45 minutes		**Close Reading Lesson** (Fluency included): 30 minutes; **Read-Aloud:** 15 minutes		

Writing Lesson: 30 minutes
Small Groups: 30–60 minutes

- Next, my writing lesson integrates word recognition and language comprehension. It follows the close-reading lesson because students write about what they read.
- Small-group instruction also integrates word recognition and language comprehension, as students work on activities that address both. Often, I spend a bit more time on word recognition because some students require additional support in that area, particularly those participating in small groups focused on decoding (see page 116).
- Finally, the read-aloud is a time for my students to enjoy a beautiful story or informational text, and strengthen language comprehension.

Fluency is a bridge between word recognition and language comprehension. I dedicate time for fluency practice in my phonics lesson, when students apply their newly learned phonics skill to a decodable text. I also dedicate time for fluency practice in my close-reading lesson, when we engage in choral-reading and partner-reading of a grade-level text. Starting around February of first grade, I engage students in a fluency practice called Partner Reading Paragraph Shrinking (see *7 Mighty Moves*, page 123). By this time, I'm usually comfortable dedicating 30 minutes to our phonics lessons, instead of 45 minutes, or reducing our small-group time by about 15 minutes. I use those extra minutes on this fluency-building activity.

Should Phonics Lessons Be Taught Whole Class or Small Group?

I deliver the majority of instruction to the whole class, including my phonics lessons. Then I use small-group time to reinforce concepts I taught, provide practice opportunities, and give immediate, individualized feedback. I prefer teaching phonics lessons to the whole class for the following reasons:

1. My phonics instruction is my superpower. I have strong routines, clear instructions, and good management, and I keep a quick pace. My students thrive during these lessons, and I want all my students to experience them.
2. When I look at class data, the majority of my students show above-average growth in reading, so I know my instruction is working.
3. While recognizing the wide range of abilities in any classroom, I find many of the needs of K–1 students to be more common than varied. For example, I start first grade with a review of the alphabet. I find that even students who have mastered the alphabet often struggle with correct letter formation, and the review helps.
4. Phonics instruction is about more than learning to read words. It's also about learning to spell words and use them in sentences. My advanced readers often need instruction and support in spelling the graphemes they are able to read. For example, they may be able to read words such as *snack* and *shouted*, but struggle to spell them. If I placed them further along in my phonics scope and sequence, they may miss out on some important spelling concepts.
5. When I teach *all* my students, I become more aware of how they are progressing, as well as what they are learning. What I observe during my phonics lessons helps me as I work with them throughout the day.
6. I embed handwriting instruction during this time, which benefits all students.
7. Students receive my consistent language and feedback as I reinforce what I taught in the morning's phonics lesson throughout the day. For example, I point out words that contain our targeted grapheme during other parts of the day, such as close reading and writing.
8. I can challenge advanced readers by having them read and spell multisyllabic words that contain the targeted grapheme. I can provide further extension during small-group time by giving them appropriately challenging texts.
9. I can give struggling students more attention and prompting during whole-class lessons. I also give them extra practice on the same concepts during small-group time. This double dose helps them stay on track, and not fall behind.
10. If I do not teach the whole class, there is the potential for inconsistent, ineffective instruction led by well-intentioned paraprofessionals who have less knowledge and training, and may struggle to manage student behaviors.

Some teachers I know do not devote time to whole-class phonics instruction. Instead, they follow a "Walk to Read" model, where they group students at various points along a phonics scope and sequence. Students then "walk" to the classroom or space where they receive a phonics lesson tailored to their needs. Often additional teachers or paraprofessionals are recruited so students receive even more precise differentiated small-group instruction. This can be an effective way to address students' needs if your school has the resources to take on this approach.

Both methods can work if done well. Do what works best for you and your students.

FIRST- AND SECOND-GRADE SCHEDULES

What does my literacy block actually look like across the week? Here's my typical full-day schedule for first and second grades.

Full-Day Schedule for First Grade and Second Grade

	Monday	Tuesday	Wednesday	Thursday	Friday
8:50	Arrival	Arrival	Arrival	Arrival	Arrival
9:00	Phonics	Phonics	Phonics	Phonics	Phonics
9:45	Close Reading	Close Reading	Close Reading	Close Reading	Close Reading
10:15	Recess	Recess	Recess	Recess	Recess
10:30	Writing	Writing	Writing	Writing	Writing
11:00	Small Groups	Small Groups	Small Groups	Small Groups	Small Groups
12:00	Lunch	Lunch	Lunch	Lunch	Lunch
12:35	Read-Aloud	Read-Aloud	Read-Aloud	Read-Aloud	Read-Aloud
12:50	PE	Computers	Library (to 1:20) 1:20–1:50 Music or Counselor (rotating weeks)	Art	Math
1:40	Math	Math	Math	Math	1:30: Early Dismissal
2:15	Recess	Recess	Recess	Recess	
2:30	Math	Math	Math	Math	
2:55	Science/Social Studies	Science/Social Studies	Science/Social Studies	Science/Social Studies	
3:25	Pack Up	Pack Up	Pack Up	Pack Up	
3:30	Dismissal	Dismissal	Dismissal	Dismissal	

Have Only 90 Minutes? Here's What I Suggest...

If you have only 90 minutes for your literacy block and no way to increase the time, spend 30 minutes on foundational skills (phonemic awareness and phonics), 30 minutes on close reading, and 30 minutes on small groups, and embed writing instruction in your science and/or social studies lessons.

The order of components might change from year to year, depending on how and when my administrators plan recess, specials, and lunch, as well as availability of a paraprofessional and Tier 2 intervention time. Even when the order changes, though, I try to preserve the time allotment for each section. This year, for example, I moved my small-group time to immediately after arrival because that is when I was scheduled to have a paraprofessional. It is also when some of my students receive Tier 2 intervention for 30 minutes (from 9:00–9:30). Furthermore, I split my phonics lesson into two parts because of when recess was scheduled. The order of components is not as important as the time you devote to each one.

This alternate schedule illustrates a different order of components and how I reduce small-group time in the spring to incorporate a fluency-building protocol called Partner Reading Paragraph Shrinking (see *7 Mighty Moves*, page 123).

Alternate Schedule That Incorporates Fluency Instruction

	Monday	Tuesday	Wednesday	Thursday	Friday
8:50	Arrival	Arrival	Arrival	Arrival	Arrival
9:00	Small Groups	Small Groups	Small Groups	Small Groups	Small Groups
9:45	Phonics		Phonics		
10:00		Phonics		Phonics	Phonics
10:25	Recess	Recess	Recess	Recess	Recess
10:40	Fluency	Phonics	Fluency	Phonics	Fluency
11:00	Close Reading	Close Reading	Close Reading	Close Reading	Close Reading
11:30	Writing	Writing	Writing	Writing	Writing
12:00	Lunch	Lunch	Lunch	Lunch	Lunch
12:35	Read-Aloud	Read-Aloud	Read-Aloud	Read-Aloud	Read-Aloud

WIN Time

Many schools allocate a specific time for intervention or extension activities, often called "What I Need" or "WIN" time. During WIN time, classes are divided into small groups, and students in each group receive targeted instruction based on their individual needs. WIN time is meant to supplement, rather than replace, core Tier 1 literacy instruction.

In some years, my WIN time has been scheduled in the afternoon, and in others, it has been scheduled during my morning literacy block. When it's been in the afternoon, I've had to adjust the timing of read-aloud, math, and science/social studies to accommodate it. When it's been scheduled in the morning, intervention paraprofessionals work with some students during the initial 30 minutes of our small-group time. I then meet with the same students in small group when they return to the classroom. Regardless of when WIN time is scheduled, I prioritize providing participating students with small-group differentiated instruction from me and intervention from the paraprofessional. To ensure adequate time for this dual support, I allot 45 to 60 minutes for small-group instruction.

KINDERGARTEN SCHEDULE

The schedules on pages 17 and 18 work well for first and second grades, but kindergarten is a whole different ballgame! Full disclosure, when I taught kindergarten, my "day" ended shortly before lunch! Teaching half-day kindergarten definitely had its challenges, but it's also where I learned to make the most of every minute. Since then, my district has switched to full-day kindergarten and I'm envious of those added minutes. I have not tested the following schedule, but it's what I'd use if I moved back to kindergarten—and, of course, adjust as necessary once the year got underway.

Full-Day Schedule for Kindergarten

	Monday	Tuesday	Wednesday	Thursday	Friday
8:50	Arrival	Arrival	Arrival	Arrival	Arrival
9:00	Show and Tell	Show and Tell	Show and Tell	Show and Tell	Show and Tell
9:10	Phonics	Phonics	Phonics	Phonics	Phonics
9:55	Close Reading	Close Reading	Close Reading	Close Reading	Close Reading
10:25	Recess	Recess	Recess	Recess	Recess
10:40	Centers	Centers	Centers	Centers	Centers
11:40	Lunch	Lunch	Lunch	Lunch	Lunch
12:15	Writing	Writing	Writing	Writing	Math
12:35	Math	Math	Math	Math	Math
1:05	Math Centers	Math Centers	Math Centers	Math Centers	Special Activity
1:30	Science/Social Studies	Science/Social Studies	Science/Social Studies	Science/Social Studies	1:30 Early Dismissal
2:00	Snack Time and Social Skills	Snack Time and Social Skills	Snack Time and Social Skills	Snack Time and Social Skills	
2:15	Recess	Recess	Recess	Recess	
2:30	PE	Music	Art	Library	
3:10	Read-Aloud	Read-Aloud	Read-Aloud	Read-Aloud	
3:30	Dismissal	Dismissal	Dismissal	Dismissal	

MAKING THE MOST OF EVERY MINUTE

While it's important to allocate a significant amount of time every day to your literacy block, *how* you use that time is what's most critical. Think about how you use those precious minutes because your planned time and actual teaching time may differ significantly.

- Did you spend a couple minutes looking for your manual?
- How long did it take students to move from the rug to their desks during the phonics lesson?
- Did a missing marker interrupt your lesson?
- Did an office aide stop by to pass on a message?
- Did you need to speak to a few students whispering in the back of the room?
- Was your pacing prohibiting you from getting to all the parts of the lesson?
- Were some students "off-task" or daydreaming during the lesson?

Researchers refer to the time students are engaged in tasks that lead to learning as academic learning time (ALT), and have found a shortage of it in classrooms.

Those lost minutes add up, and suddenly students aren't receiving the full amount of instructional time you planned for them. And if that is happening every day, throughout the day, students may be missing several days' worth of instruction by the year's end. Researchers refer to the time students are engaged in tasks that lead to learning as academic learning time (ALT), and have found a shortage of it in classrooms. What many teachers plan and what they actually do can be very different (Smith et al., 2001). Let's explore some ways to maximize the amount of academic learning time our students receive.

Routines and Procedures

You can make the most of every minute by establishing consistent routines and following clear procedures. When we establish routines and follow procedures, students can focus on what they are learning, rather than on what they are supposed to be doing. I'll explain routines and procedures for each component of my block in the chapters to come.

Established routines and procedures are particularly important to ensure smooth transitions. Think about all the transitions that happen during a lesson. Sometimes they are large, such as when students move from one part of the room to another, and sometimes they are small, such as when students get out their individual dry-erase boards, open a book, or put folders away. It's easy to lose academic learning time during those moments, so it's important to have tight transitions in place that require as little direction as possible from you. Take time to carefully consider the transitions in your lessons and how you can improve their flow. Then teach students step-by-step procedures for the transition, and allow plenty of time for them to practice.

BEHIND THE SCENES

Practicing Transitions

Transitions should be quick and efficient, but that won't happen on its own. So spend a lot of time practicing them at the beginning of the year. Go slow to go fast! And, if necessary, don't be afraid to stop students to practice a transition again. Of course, that might mean you don't get through all the parts of a lesson initially. But taking the extra time to teach transitions explicitly at the beginning of the year will pay off in the rest of year. Your lessons will be much more efficient and effective.

Delivering Instruction

The way we deliver instruction can have a massive impact on student learning. Much of my understanding of effective teaching is rooted in Anita Archer's work, particularly her book *Explicit Instruction: Effective and Efficient Teaching*, which she co-authored with Charles Hughes (2010). Familiarizing yourself with the principles in their book can have a profound effect on the way you teach. Let's look at four suggestions that Archer and Hughes offer to improve the way we deliver instruction.

ELICIT FREQUENT RESPONSES

I keep my students engaged during lessons by allowing many opportunities for them to respond, which significantly enhances learning outcomes. It also increases their time on task and helps to reduce disruptive behaviors (MacSuga-Gage & Simonsen, 2015). Boost learning and decrease disruptions? Sounds like a win-win to me! There are many ways students can respond:

Verbal Responses: Students can verbally respond to your questions. If the answers are short and the same, allow students to answer chorally. Give a signal that lets students know when they can respond. For example, when I ask a question, I lift my hand up to my head to remind students to think about it first. When I lower my hand with my palm up, students respond. I might ask, "Do we use *-ck* after a short vowel or long vowel?" Once I've lifted and lowered my hand, students say, "short vowel" in unison. If the answers are longer and more varied, students turn and discuss them with a partner or in a group.

Written Responses: Students can write short responses on individual dry-erase boards or paper. For example, I may have them write words that capture the phonics concept they're learning. Or I may have them draw a quick picture to help reinforce the meaning of a new vocabulary word.

Physical Responses: Students can point, gesture, or use a facial expression or hand signal. For example, I have students use a finger to track the text in front of them, while I read it aloud. Or I might say, "Yesterday, we learned the word *melancholy*. Use your face to show me how you might feel if you were melancholy." Or "Show me on your fingers how many sounds are in the word *they*."

Archer suggests aiming for 3–5 simple responses, such as choral responses or hand gestures, per minute. For more complex responses, such as partner sharing or a written answer, she suggests at least one response per minute. For very complex or involved responses, such as writing to a prompt, she suggests one every 10–30 minutes.

No "Opting Out"

Too often, students opt out of lessons, meaning they go off-task, day dream, or become disengaged. But, as Anita Archer says, "Learning is not a spectator sport" (2022). Expecting students to respond frequently requires them to pay attention and participate. I find that if I go on and on, without inviting students to respond, they lose interest. But I can easily change that by involving all students in my lessons.

Monitoring students and providing feedback is a critical part of instruction.

MONITOR STUDENTS

Even if we are teaching at the front of the room, we need to be aware of what is happening throughout the room, especially at the back. We need to observe students carefully and offer feedback and gentle corrections when necessary. Additionally, I don't advise remaining at the front of the room for the whole lesson. Instead, monitor students by circulating through the room. As they respond in writing, for example, walk around to observe their work and offer guidance and feedback.

PROVIDE FEEDBACK

Providing clear, constructive feedback is essential for student growth. It's especially important to correct students' errors immediately so they aren't reinforced by repeating the same mistake. There are three types of feedback: affirmative, informative, and corrective:

- **Affirmative:** Praise your students for a job well done. Be specific so they know exactly what they did well. "I love how you remembered a finger-space between your words." Or "I'm grateful to Diego for looking right at me. I can tell he's ready to learn."

- **Informative:** Tell students what they can improve upon. "You have a great sentence here that shares important information with your reader. To make it even better, you could begin with a linking word or phrase. Can you think of a linking word or phrase that would work here?"
- **Corrective:** Ask students to fix an error in their work. "Oops, look carefully. The word is *sit*. You wrote *set*. Which letter do you need to change?" Or "When you form the letter *h*, you need to start at the top not at the bottom. Watch me: tall down, roll down, *h*. Try again." Or ask them to change a behavior. I might say, "Turn all the way around and make sure you are facing me." Or "Please put the toy away and get out your marker."

KEEP A BRISK PACE

Maintaining a brisk pace is key to keeping students engaged in instruction. We can't move too quickly or too slowly. We should strike a balance between allowing students sufficient think time and opportunities to respond, and keeping things moving. This prevents boredom and ensures students are actively participating. Establishing instructional routines and being prepared can help keep your pace on track.

Also, try to avoid digressions while you're teaching. While it's fun to share personal observations and stories, you should do it strategically to reinforce learning. We all know children love to raise their hands and share something completely unrelated to what is happening in the classroom. I often motion those students to lower their hands and share at a better point in the day.

BEHIND THE SCENES

Managing Bathroom Breaks

If students need to use the bathroom, they give me a signal: They raise their hand with their index and middle fingers crossed. I nod my head, and they quietly slip out of the classroom without disrupting classmates. This method allows me to continue on with instruction and prevents the domino effect of everyone suddenly asking to go.

Preparing for Instruction

Another way to increase your students' academic learning time is to be as prepared as possible. Now, I know you already plan and read through your lessons before school, but there are additional ways to prepare. Do you have all the materials ready to go? Find the phoneme-grapheme cards, vocabulary cards, and high-frequency word cards before the lesson begins; prewrite the words you'll have students read together; get your slides up and ready to present, etc. There will always be rushed mornings when you aren't fully prepared, but try to fit in those tasks and others like them, as often as possible.

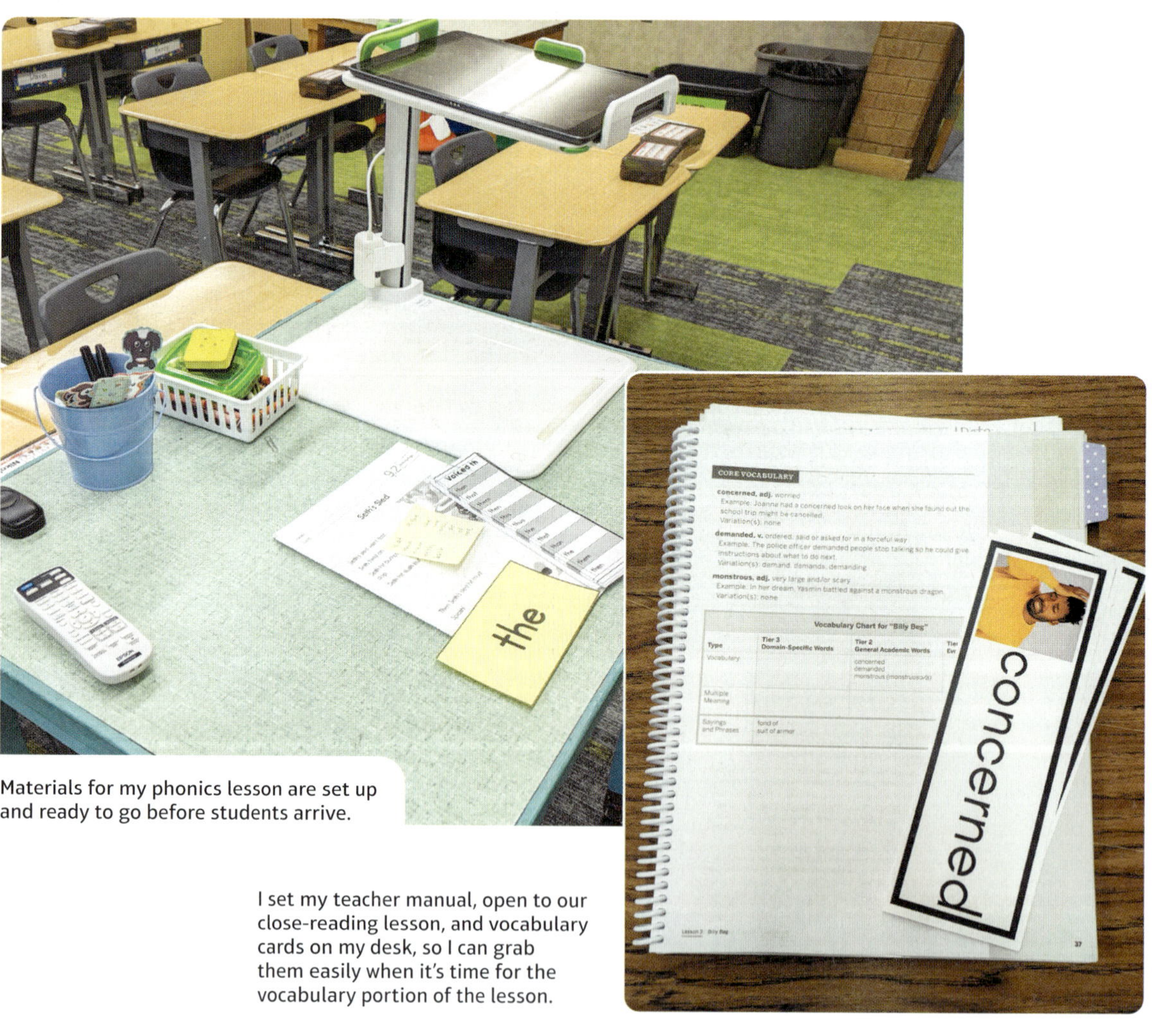

Materials for my phonics lesson are set up and ready to go before students arrive.

I set my teacher manual, open to our close-reading lesson, and vocabulary cards on my desk, so I can grab them easily when it's time for the vocabulary portion of the lesson.

My first small-group lesson of the day is prepped and ready to go before we begin. I collect grapheme cards, words lists, and books so that I don't have to go hunting during valuable learning time. I also prewrite the words from the book that I want to review.

I prewrite the words my students and I will read together on a magnetic handwriting mat, which I move to my easel when we're ready for that part of the lesson. I place grapheme cards and the teacher manual behind the easel for easy access.

BEHIND THE SCENES
Prepping Materials

I stay at least a week ahead in prepping materials and making them ready to go. I use these bins to organize all the materials I need for the week.

A WORD OF ENCOURAGEMENT

While the details and schedules I share in this chapter work for me, they may not work for you. So many factors come into play when it comes to teaching, such as your available time, your instructional practices and pacing, your programs and materials, your students' engagement, your classroom-management strategies, and the individual needs of your students. So feel free to modify the details and schedules I offer.

It really does come down to *your* students and their needs. So how do you know if what you're doing is effective? That's where assessment comes in.

Assessing Students

Assessment is a useful tool to determine if the way we've structured our block is effective. For example, one year the disappointing results of my mid-year reading screener, Acadience, gave me pause. I was implementing evidence-aligned practices, so why wasn't my instruction working as I expected it to? It was working for most of my students, but not all of them, and it needed to. What could I do about it?

Because my instruction was working for most of the kids, I decided to increase the dosage of instruction for only the kids who needed it. But how could I find extra time to work with them in my already packed day? I restructured my small-group instruction and enlisted parent volunteers to help, which gave me more time with the students who needed extra support. Then I monitored their progress carefully to see if these changes had the desired effect. They did! I was relieved to see their reading skills improve.

If we don't do anything with the data, there is no point in giving the assessment in the first place! Let the data guide you.

Administering assessments is only the first step. We need to evaluate the results and adjust our instruction accordingly. Analyzing and responding to data is at the core of the science of reading! The key here is to be responsive. If we don't do anything with the data, there is no point in giving the assessment in the first place! Let the data guide you.

When analyzing data, we can identify not only patterns of individual students, but also patterns of the whole class. The broader patterns we identify can help us determine if the literacy block's structure, as well as our instruction, is working. I always strive to ensure I'm using my classroom time as effectively as possible. I reflect on my students' progress, or lack thereof, and look at the data. Are the majority of my students making above-average growth? If so, then I need not worry. However, I also maintain an open mind, knowing there is always potential for improvement.

As you analyze your data and consider the unique needs of your students, you may find that a different structure works better for your literacy block from the one I describe in this book—and that's okay. For example, while I prefer to teach whole-class phonics lessons, you may find it more beneficial to place students in small groups at various points along the phonics scope and sequence, especially in second grade, when individual differences in phonics skills may become more pronounced. Never let my schedule, your schedule, or someone else's schedule dictate what your students need. Let data drive your decisions. Do what works best for you and your students.

TYPES OF ASSESSMENT

There are different types of assessment with different purposes that can assist us in planning instruction:

- A ***universal screening assessment*** tells me who is on track to meet grade-level goals and who is not. I administer this assessment three times a year, at the beginning, middle, and end of the year.
- For students who are not on track, I can dive deeper with a ***diagnostic assessment***, which tells me where the student is having difficulty and exactly what skills they need help with. From there, I plan my instruction based on that data. For example, after giving a phonics diagnostic, I learn that my student struggles with words with *-ng* and *-nk*. Now I know that I need to reteach that concept to that student.

Assessments I Rely On

I use Acadience (formerly known as Dibels Next) for my universal screening and progress monitoring assessments. There is such a deep research base behind this tool. It doesn't take long for me to assess each student, and I find the results to be accurate.

For the diagnostic assessment, I find the *CORE Phonics Survey* and *LETRS Phonics and Word Reading Survey* to be solid options.

- I use ***progress monitoring assessments*** throughout the year to see if my instruction, or a particular intervention, is working. Say I begin a fluency intervention for a student. I can monitor his or her progress by administering a timed oral reading fluency assessment. By assessing the student again every week or every other week, I can look at his or her rate of improvement to determine if the intervention is effective or if I need to adjust it. Administering this type of test frequently allows me to see patterns more quickly so I can judge if the student is making adequate progress.
- In addition to those more formal assessments, I rely on ***informal assessments***. I listen and observe my students during my whole-class lessons, as well as small-group instruction. I walk around during the dictation portion of our phonics lessons to determine who needs help. I evaluate my students' writing closely to see if they are applying the skills I've taught them.

In Closing, Remember...

The literacy block is a crucial part of your day. Effective planning involves determining how much time in your day it will occupy and allocating sufficient time for each component. However, *how* you use that time is even more important. Maximizing student engagement requires thorough preparation, predictable routines, and, of course, effective instruction.

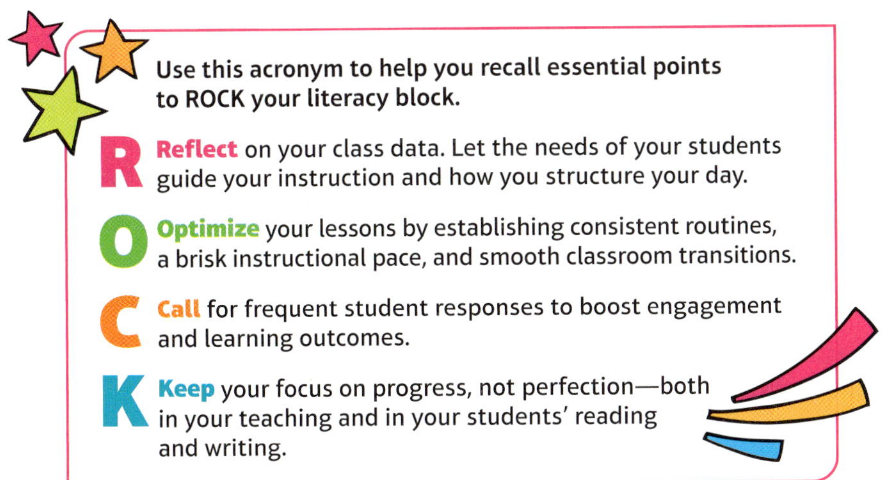

When planning your literacy block, carefully consider these questions:

- How many minutes will I devote to my literacy block and to each component?
- Is there a big difference in my planned teaching time and students' actual learning time? If so, how can I decrease that difference?
- What routines and procedures do I currently use and where could I build some in?
- What elements of effective instruction am I embracing and what elements am I not and, therefore, need to work on?

Remember, what I share in this book is just one way to organize a literacy block. Your block does not need to look exactly like mine, and that's perfectly fine. Consider this book a glimpse into my practice, designed to help you assess your approach and inspire your own good ideas.

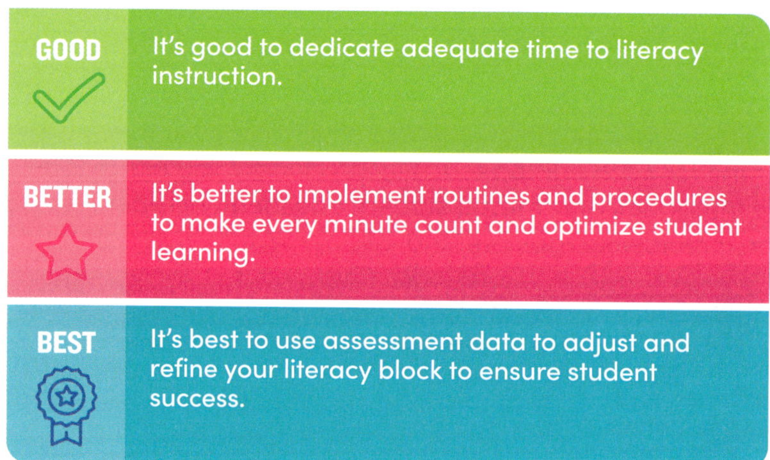

Curtain Up: Arrival

CHAPTER 2

SPOTLIGHT ON ARRIVAL

Once the morning bell rings, I set aside all my prep and planning duties to greet students as they enter the classroom. The students come in, hang up their backpacks and coats, turn in their take-home folders, and then sit on the rug. We chat until everyone has put their things away and gotten settled. I then lead the class in our morning chant to start the day. Next, we read the morning message together and discuss it. Then we celebrate students who have reached a milestone in our reading software program. After school announcements and the pledge, we dive into our phonics lesson.

DOMINANT MOVE FROM *7 MIGHTY MOVES*

MOVE 1: Teach Phonemic Awareness With Intention

A Closer Look at Each Step

Let's take a closer look at the routine, which takes around 10 minutes each day, by focusing on what the students and I do upon their arrival to school.

Lindsay Live! Enter her classroom to learn more about arrival.

1 UNPACKING AND SETTLING IN

Backpack area, 3–5 minutes

The arrival routine sets the mood and atmosphere for the rest of the school day. It's always tempting for me to squeeze in some last-minute prep and planning for the day, but once the bell rings and students start entering the classroom, I set all that aside to be present for them. I greet them with a cheerful smile as they enter the room. As they hang up their backpacks and put their take-home folders in the basket near the door, I chat with some of them, asking about their morning or an event in their lives, such as their birthday party, dance recital, or latest soccer game.

Arrival Routine Steps

1. Unpacking
2. Welcome Chant
3. Morning Message
4. Announcements

Students hang up their coats and backpacks on their assigned hooks.

While these interactions might appear insignificant, they're a deliberate part of my morning routine. When I begin the day attending to students' well-being and creating a welcoming environment, it reduces friction throughout the day and allows me to maintain the flow of instruction and more easily guide student behaviors. In fact, research shows that regular positive interactions with students are great ways to proactively manage classroom behavior (Cook et al., 2016).

BEHIND THE SCENES

Transporting Papers

I provide each student with a folder to transport papers between home and school, reducing the risk of parent notes and assignments getting lost.

I acknowledge students' positive behavior and performance, and engage them in conversations, starting from the beginning of the day. Those moves are backed by research that shows that increased praise during instruction boosts student engagement, focus, and learning (Sutherland et al., 2000). I've learned that my feedback should be specific and clear to reinforce the desired behaviors and help students understand exactly what they did well. Additionally, I strive to ensure that I have more positive interactions with students than negative ones. That's because our attention instinctively gets drawn to disruptive or inappropriate behaviors, and how we respond to these behaviors is often a correction that results in a negative interaction, such as shaking your head no, or telling a student to stop guessing when reading. Aiming for a 5:1 ratio of positive-to-negative interactions with students will increase the amount of engaged academic time and reduce unwanted behaviors (Cook et al., 2016).

In addition to boosting engagement, focus, and learning, a positive arrival routine helps me build meaningful relationships with my students, giving them a sense of belonging that enhances their overall well-being. I want students to thrive! I want them to feel loved and cared for.

Having intentional conversations with students is not only good for building relationships but also developing language skills (Cabell et al., 2015). Strive for five conversation turns, or exchanges, when talking with students, rather than just a couple. For example, if you ask an open-ended question ("How was your weekend?"), and the child responds ("Good."), then you respond by prompting him or her with another question ("What was the best thing about it?"). The child responds ("I went to my grandma's house and played with my cousins."), and finally, you expand on his or her response ("Oh, how fun! I have such fond memories of spending time with my cousins when I was little. We loved playing hide-and-seek together!"). For many more examples of strive-for-five conversations, check out Tricia Zucker and Sonia Cabell's book.

As you engage in strive-for-five conversations, consider also the behavior-management strategy "Two-by-Ten" with students who are exhibiting challenging behaviors or who may benefit from additional emotional support. Implementing this strategy is easy—just commit to engaging the student in a two-minute conversation each day, for ten consecutive days. Doing that will improve the student's behavior and her relationship with you (Wlodkowski, 1983; Woolf, 2024). I've found that arrival time is perfect for engaging in these brief check-ins.

2 WELCOME CHANT

Whole class, on the rug, 1 minute

After unpacking, students make their way to the rug, where I'm sitting in my rocking chair. I assign seats on the rug to enhance focus, promote positive peer interactions, and create a more orderly and manageable learning environment. I carefully consider students' needs as I decide who will sit where. I place students who need more academic or behavior support in the front row so I can easily monitor and assist them when needed. We start things off with a song or a chant.

Chanting or singing together fosters a sense of community and belonging. It lifts our spirits and signals that it's time to start our day of learning.

3 MORNING MESSAGE

Whole class, on the rug, 3–4 minutes

Next up is our morning message. Every morning before school, I write a short message on my whiteboard easel, such as an announcement, a review of past lessons, a discussion question, or a reminder about classroom rules. To reinforce phonemic awareness and letter-sound relationships, I use a technique called "dot and dash" that I learned from Nora Chahbazi, creator of the Evidence-Based Literacy Instruction (EBLI) program. I draw students' attention to each word in the message. If one letter represents a sound, I put a dot underneath it, using a dry-erase marker, while I say the sound. If two or more letters represent a sound, I underline them, or "dash" them, while I say

the sound. Students echo each sound, and then we blend them together to form the word. Then we move onto the next word.

For example, for the word *dear*, the instruction might look like this:

I say, /d/ while putting a dot under the *d*.
Students say, /d/.
I say, /ea/ while underlining the *ea*.
Students say, /ea/.
I say, /r/ while putting a dot under the *r*.
Students say, /r/.
I say, *dear* while scooping the entire word with my marker.
Students say, *dear*. Then I go on to the next word.

After reading each word by segmenting its sounds and blending them, we read the entire message together fluently. At the beginning of the year, I say the sounds first and have the students echo me. Later in the year, the students and I say the sounds and words together and, eventually, they do it without me.

There are several reasons why I like this activity:

- It builds the critical phonemic awareness skills of blending and segmenting. I'm helping students segment the sounds in a word and then blend them back together. These skills directly impact reading and writing.
- It develops phonemic awareness using letters. I'm drawing students' attention to the letters as I dot and dash them while we blend and segment. It shows students how the sounds we hear connect with the letters they see.
- It helps to reinforce phonics skills I've taught, as well as preview some advanced phonics skills that students haven't learned yet. I love giving these sneak peeks because some astute students will begin to recognize these new patterns and even apply their knowledge as they read and write.
- It discourages whole-word visual memorization of words. This activity slows students down a bit, enabling them to attend to the sounds in words.

Now, I don't require students to read this way the rest of the day if they are ready to read words with automaticity. Certainly at other times, we are working on fluent reading. But during morning message, the focus is on phonemic awareness by segmenting and blending each word.

It's satisfying to watch students' reading progress. At the beginning of the year, usually no student is able to read the message independently. By December, most students are rushing to the morning message before we begin to see if they can read it on their own. It is so rewarding when they proudly beam at me and announce, "I know what it says!"

After we finish reading the morning message, we take some time to discuss it. I might elaborate on the message by providing additional information or prompting students to discuss it with a partner before sharing their thoughts as a class. To support students' oral language development, it's important to infuse language into everything we do (Cardenas-Hagan, 2024).

4 ANNOUNCEMENTS

Whole class, on the rug, 1–3 minutes

We listen to school announcements on the intercom and then I share any additional news. I recognize students who have reached a milestone in our reading software program by giving them their certificate, and everyone applauds. Students love this recognition and are motivated by it. I find they work harder and stay focused during technology center time. On Mondays, I assign classroom jobs for the week (see box to the right).

Now we are ready to move into our phonics lesson.

TRANSITION TIP

Prep for Phonics

While students are listening to the school announcements, I erase the whiteboard and pick up my phonics manual in preparation for our upcoming lesson.

BEHIND THE SCENES

Assigning Jobs

I used to change classroom-job assignments daily, but found it was much too time-consuming. So I simplified things by designating only two helpers each week to do all jobs (holding the door open, wiping lunchroom tables, etc.).

In Closing, Remember...

The arrival routine sets the mood and atmosphere for the rest of the school day. Start strong by initiating positive interactions with your students. This not only prevents disruptive behaviors but also cultivates a calm, productive learning environment. Engaging in purposeful conversations with students further strengthens your relationships with them and enhances their language development. Additionally, you can put a twist on the traditional morning message by looking at it through a phonemic awareness lens. It's a great way to boost students' blending and segmenting abilities, while also introducing a topic for discussion.

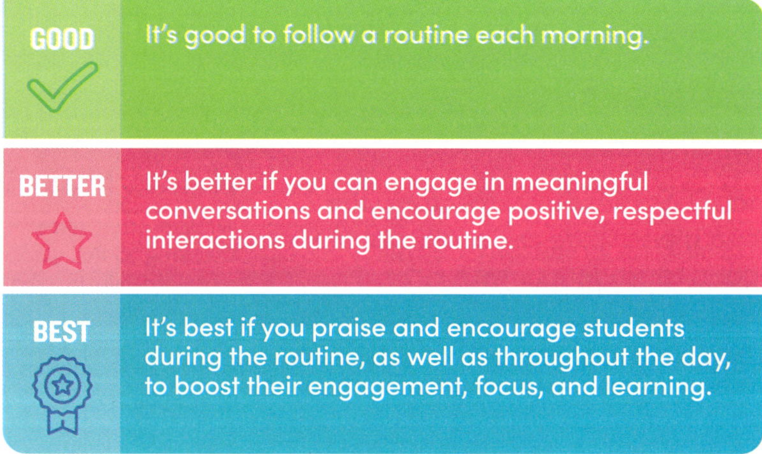

Sound Check: Phonics

CHAPTER 3

SPOTLIGHT ON PHONICS

After arrival, I launch into the phonics lesson, which moves briskly from a phonemic awareness warm-up to reading and writing target words to reading a decodable text. Within this lesson, you'll see students responding as a whole class, reading together, and reading individually—they also move from the rug to their desks. The planning, materials preparation, and transitions I do make the lesson run smoothly. Come take a closer look!

DOMINANT MOVES FROM *7 MIGHTY MOVES*

MOVE 1: Teach Phonemic Awareness With Intention

MOVE 2: Teach Phonics Explicitly and Systematically

MOVE 3: Teach Decoding Strategies, Not Cueing Strategies

MOVE 4: Use Decodable Texts Instead of Predictable Texts With Beginning Readers

MOVE 5: Embrace a Better Approach to Teaching "Sight Words"

Explicit and systematic phonics instruction is essential for unlocking the code and developing proficient readers. Earlier in my career, I overlooked the importance of this foundational skill and expected students to figure it out on their own. I didn't understand what good phonics instruction looked like. Now, I've witnessed firsthand the impact explicit phonics instruction has on my students. By systematically following a scope and sequence of phonics skills, we can equip students with the tools they need to decode text and enable them to become confident and skilled readers and writers.

Lindsay Live! Enter her classroom to learn more about phonics.

The phonics lesson is the most structured part of my literacy block. It follows a steady and specific series of routines. Don't underestimate the power of consistent routines! You might worry that students will become bored by such routines, but I find they thrive with this consistency. They become more confident because they know exactly what to expect. Once the routines become habit, they can spend their cognitive energy on the new concept I'm teaching. Additionally, they are less likely to act out or become anxious. Step into my classroom during this time and you'll be greeted by a buzz of accomplishment. Joy and learning can and do coexist, even with these very structured routines.

Another consideration, as you plan your phonics lesson, is where the students are situated and how you transition them from one lesson step to another. It's important to keep the transitions as tight as possible, so as not to interrupt the lesson's flow and to maximize the amount of learning time for students. Each minute is precious!

Phonics Lesson Steps

1. Phonemic Awareness Warm-Up
2. Review
3. New Concept Introduction
4. Choral Word Reading
5. Word Dictation
6. Sentence Dictation
7. High-Frequency Word Instruction
8. Partner Word Reading
9. Decodable Text Reading
10. Close

Feel free to change the order of steps so the lesson structure works for you and the flow of your instruction.

A Closer Look at Each Step

Let's delve into the lesson steps, focusing on the details of my instruction, the physical spaces in which we work, and the transitions between the steps.

There are several reasons I like to begin our phonics lesson on the rug. The rug is a welcoming and convenient starting point for our day. I can easily transition from greeting students and sharing announcements to the phonics lesson since we're already gathered. I love this close-knit arrangement. Huddled together, the students seem to focus better. They are more manageable and more likely to give me eye contact, which allows me to ensure everyone is paying attention. During our phonemic awareness warm-up, I can hear their voices more clearly, and I can instantly respond when someone incorrectly segments a word. As I explain a new concept, I can more easily determine if they understand it. When students turn and talk to ask and answer questions and explain a concept to one another, I can lean in and listen.

TRANSITION TIP

Prep Materials

Before students arrive in the morning, I lay out all the materials I need for the rug activities so I can grab them swiftly. Those materials include:

- Phonics manual, opened to the correct page
- Phoneme-grapheme cards, organized for various review drills
- Blending board (or easel)

BEHIND THE SCENES

Finding a "Just Right" Pace

The key to keeping students engaged is finding a "just right" pace—not too slow, not too fast. Dragging out steps can quickly lose students' attention, while rushing through steps can leave them scrambling to catch up. A brisk, well-paced lesson maximizes learning while allowing time to process information and practice new skills. Finding that sweet spot takes time and requires attention to all learners.

1 PHONEMIC AWARENESS WARM-UP

Whole class, on the rug, 1–3 minutes

I prepare students for phonics by having them tune in to the sounds of spoken words. I focus on blending and segmenting individual phonemes because those tasks help them both read and write words.

The routine begins with the blending song. Then I segment words for students, while they blend them into a word. Here's what it might look like:

1. I sing, "Slide, slide, slippity slide. When I say the sounds, you're gonna make 'em glide."
2. I say, /ch/ /i/ /p/. Students say, "chip."
3. I say, /s/ /u/ /ch/. Students say, "such."
4. Repeat with 5–6 more words.

The routine continues with the segmenting song written by Erica Allen-Jamison.

5. I sing, "Break it down, break it down." (Snap in between the phrases)

   "Break it down, break it down, break it down." (Said more quickly, arms crossing and tapping legs)

   "I say the words, you say the sounds."

   "Break it down." (Arms crossing and tapping legs)

6. I say, "chat." Students say, /ch/ /a/ /t/.
7. I say, "much." Students say, /m/ /u/ /ch/.
8. Repeat with 5–6 more words.

For this warm-up, I use words directly from our phonics lesson, which we'll read and spell later. Keep the warm-up brief, just a few minutes, and focus on two skills at a time (Erbeli et al., 2024; National Reading Panel, 2000). If some students need additional phonemic awareness support, provide further practice during small-group instruction.

② REVIEW

Whole class, on the rug, 5 minutes

Immediately following our warm-up, I grab the pack of phoneme-grapheme cards (cards with a grapheme, or spelling, on the front), and move into a phonics review, typically in three parts: visual drill, blending drill, and auditory drill. Let's look at each one.

Visual Drill

I use 25–30 cards that feature graphemes (spellings) students have learned. I flip through the cards, pausing as they say the sound(s), or phonemes, that each grapheme represents. This is a quick drill, only about 1–2 minutes.

BEHIND THE SCENES

Correcting Errors

Because we're on the rug, students can easily see the cards and say the sounds as I flip through them. If they say a sound incorrectly, I immediately correct them and put the card back in the stack so students have another chance to get it right. This immediate error correction and practice is critical to avoid reinforcing the error.

TRANSITION TIP

Prepare Phoneme-Grapheme Cards

I have two separate stacks of phoneme-grapheme cards, one for the visual drill and the other for the blending drill. That way, I can prepare the blending drill cards before school so I don't waste classroom time dividing the stack into three piles: beginning, middle, and end. I put the graphemes in a position that makes sense. For example, *x* and *ck* should always come at the end so I place them in the third pile.

Blending Drill

I point to the graphemes on my blending board as students say each sound and blend them into a word. I change one card and lead students in blending again. Sometimes I don't use the blending board and, instead, simply write the word on the whiteboard easel—especially if I've had a busy morning and didn't set up my blending board before school! Then, with my magnetic eraser, I quickly erase and replace one grapheme at a time and lead students in blending the new word. We spend about 2–3 minutes on this drill.

Auditory Drill

I say a sound, and students write all the graphemes they have learned for that sound, saying the sounds as they write. For example:

1. I say, "The sound is /sh/."
2. Students say, "/sh/; *s-h* spells /sh/" while they write it.
3. I say, "The sound is /th/."
4. Students say, "/th/; *t-h* spells /th/" while they write it.
5. I say, "The sound is /ay/."
6. Students say, "/ay/; *a* spells /ay/, a magic *e* spells /ay/, *ai* spells /ay/, *ay* spells /ay/."
7. I repeat with about five more sounds.

The downside of being on the rug is that students do not have access to writing materials for the auditory drill. Because of that, I simply have them "write" the graphemes (spellings) with a finger on the rug and then carefully monitor those who need extra help remembering the spellings. Another alternative is to move the auditory drill later in the lesson when we are at our desks, right before word dictation. This allows you to better monitor students' accuracy.

BEHIND THE SCENES

Motivating Students

To motivate students when necessary, I use the Point Game. Here's how it works:

- Put a T-chart in the corner of your whiteboard with "T" for teacher and "S" for student.
- Whenever students are engaged and following directions, they get a point on the chart.
- If they go off task or need redirection, you get a point.

This friendly competition motivates students to "beat" the teacher! It's a simple but effective way to keep them focused and engaged in learning.

3 NEW CONCEPT INTRODUCTION

Whole class, on the rug, 2–5 minutes

Before the lesson, I review the new phoneme-grapheme correspondence or phonics concept from my scope and sequence, and at the start of the lesson, explain it as clearly and succinctly as possible. I might focus on what our mouths, lips, or tongues do when we articulate the sound, and then model how to read and/or write a word that contains the targeted concept.

If we are learning a new sound, I might pass out small mirrors so students can watch their mouths as they produce the sound. Yes, I have a routine for mirror distribution! I keep a basket of mirrors nearby and give five mirrors to each "row captain," or the student at the end of each row. The row captains each take one mirror and pass the remaining four to the next student in their row. Those students each take one mirror, and pass the rest on, and so on. When it's time to put the mirrors away, we simply reverse the process, and I quickly pick up the five mirrors from each captain.

4 CHORAL WORD READING

Whole class, on the rug or at desks, 1–2 minutes

I lead students in choral-reading words that contain the target phoneme-grapheme correspondence. I either prewrite the words on the board or display them via PowerPoint. The routine I use depends on students' needs. Some of them require more scaffolding than others.

BEHIND THE SCENES

Articulation Support

Being close together on the rug, students can easily see my mouth movements as I draw attention to what my lips, teeth, and tongue are doing when I produce the sound we're talking about. The sound-spelling wall is also nearby so I can refer to it as I introduce a new spelling.

Routine 1: Continuous Blending

At the early stages, I choose words with continuous sounds (e.g., /m/ /s/ /f/) so we can stretch out each sound as we say it: /sssaaammm/ Sam. This is especially helpful for students who struggle to blend phonemes. I simply point to each letter and lead students in elongating each sound, similar to singing it, until I point to the next one, and then the next. Finally, I run my finger along the bottom of the word as we say it.

Routine 2: Successive Blending, A

Initially, words with stop sounds (e.g., /b/ /k/) can be challenging for students to blend because those sounds can't be stretched out. So I guide them in saying the sounds for the first two graphemes, blend them, and then add the ending sound. Ideally, I'd have students immediately blend the first two sounds (as in Routine 3 on page 49), but that can be difficult for students who are not yet able to blend letter sounds. This routine serves as an intermediary step between Routines 1 and 3.

Here's an example for the word *pet*.

1. I point to the *p* and say, "Sound?"
2. Students say, /p/.
3. I point to the *e* and say, "Sound?"
4. Students say, /e/.

5. I glide my finger under both the *p* and *e* and say, "Blend?"
6. Students say, /pe/. (If students can't blend two sounds together initially, I do it for them and have them repeat.)
7. I point to the *t* and say, "Sound?"
8. Students say, /t/.
9. I slide my finger under the whole word and say, "Word?"
10. Students say, "pet."
11. Repeat with about 9 more words.

As students become familiar with the routine, I can pull back my teacher voice and simply point.

TRANSITION TIP

Word Prep

Before the lesson, I write words that follow the new phonics skill on a magnetic handwriting page. That way I can move swiftly into choral-reading the words with students.

Routine 3: Successive Blending, B

As students' blending abilities and phoneme-grapheme correspondences improve, they blend the word's first two sounds right away.

Here's an example for the word *dig*.

1. I glide my finger under both the *d* and *i*, and say, "Blend?"
2. Students say, /di/.
3. I point to the *g* and say, "Sound?
4. Students say, /g/.
5. I slide my finger under the whole word and say, "Word?"
6. Students say, "dig."
7. Repeat with about 9 more words.

Again, as students become familiar with the routine, I can pull back my teacher voice and simply point to the letters.

Routine 4: Vowel Blending

This option is great for students who can blend phonemes but could use support in learning the new phonics skill.

Here's an example for *oi*.

1. I point to the *oi* and say, "Sound?"
2. Students say, /oi/
3. I say, "Word?"
4. Students say, "boil."
5. I point to the *oi* in the next word and say, "Sound?"
6. Students say, /oi/.
7. I say, "Word?"
8. Students say, "noise."
9. Repeat with about 8 more words.

TRANSITIONING FROM THE RUG TO DESKS

As you can see, the transitions between lesson steps have been rather seamless so far. They don't require much management, and their success simply relies on the teacher's preparation. But now it's time for a bigger transition where we move from the rug to desks. This transition gives students a chance to stretch their legs and release some energy before the next portion of the lesson, but it might be easy to lose the focus of the students and potentially waste valuable time. A clear transition routine ensures students stay focused. By maintaining high expectations and implementing a well-defined transition routine, we can maximize our learning time.

While we're sitting on the rug, I say "Desk, desk, desk." This cues students to immediately echo aloud, "Desk, desk, desk." Then they stand up and walk to their desks. As soon as they get there, they know to get out their individual dry-erase boards, markers, and erasers, and then wait for me to begin the Word Dictation portion of the lesson.

*** Kindergarten Note:** When I taught kindergarten, I would play an alphabet song during this transition. Not only was it fun to sing, but it also helped students learn the names and sounds of letters. The goal was to be at their desks and have their materials out by the end of the song. Now that I teach first grade, I play the alphabet song at the beginning of the year and stop after a month or so because, by then, students have a firm grip on their ABCs. You might find a different fun phonics song to play.

BEHIND THE SCENES

Setting Up Procedures

At the beginning of the year, it takes more time to set up procedures. If students struggle to move quickly from the rug to their desks, we return to the rug to try again. We practice, practice, practice the first week or so of school. That might mean we don't get through all the components of the lesson. But, as mentioned, we go slow to go fast. Taking the extra time to teach these procedures with high expectations at the beginning of the year will pay off in future weeks.

Now that students are at their desks with their dry-erase boards, markers, and erasers out, they are ready to begin the dictation portion of the lesson. It's easier to have students write while at their desks. They can practice good handwriting posture, and I can move easily and quickly between desks as I monitor their responses. After dictation, I go to the front of the room and demonstrate the high-frequency word routine on the whiteboard, while students follow along, using their dry-erase boards. Then, once again, I monitor their responses by walking around the room while they read their word lists and decodable passages with a partner.

Watch my students move swiftly from the rug to their desks.

BEHIND THE SCENES Desk Arrangement and Seat Assignments

Desk Arrangement

I've tried many different desk arrangements, but ultimately I have found that when students are facing forward, they can hear and focus better. I arrange my classroom desks in rows, with student pairs facing forward. Research suggests this configuration is more likely to help students stay on task and concentrate better (Simmons et al., 2015; Tobia et al., 2020). It facilitates partner work, while maintaining a clear line of sight of the teacher for focused learning. It also allows me to monitor and assist students more easily. When transitioning to group work, I simply have partners turn around to team up with the partners sitting behind them.

Seat Assignments

I'm strategic when it comes to seating assignments! I contemplate the needs of all my students, but give the most vulnerable ones extra consideration. I place students who frequently need assistance toward the front of the room or on the inside aisle so I can get to them easily for support and guidance. I also carefully place students who need additional focus cues or redirection in the front. I might place students who prefer to stand while they work in the back.

I also give special consideration to student pairs. We do a lot of partner work not only in our phonics lessons but also throughout the day. I partner up vulnerable students with positive peers who can offer gentle support and modeling. It requires a lot of forethought, but the extra planning pays off in a calmer and more engaged classroom for everyone.

⑤ WORD DICTATION

Whole class, at desks, 7–10 minutes

In the word dictation portion of the lesson, students practice writing words that contain the target phoneme-grapheme correspondence. Again, I follow a routine. I say each word twice, and students repeat it twice. Then they orally segment the word while tapping a finger for each sound. I share a sentence containing the word, and then students write the word while saying its sounds. Here's an example:

1. I say, "The word is *spot*, *spot*."
2. Students repeat, "*spot*, *spot*."
3. Students tap each sound with their thumb and fingers: /s/ /p/ /o/ /t/
4. I use the word in a sentence: "We found the best *spot* to have our picnic."
5. I say, "Now say the word as you write the sounds in *spot*."
6. Students spell the word while saying each sound. So for *spot*, they would say /s/ while writing the *s*, /p/ as they write the *p*, /o/ as they write the *o*, and /t/ as they write the *t*.

During word dictation, I move about the room, monitoring students' responses and correcting any errors right away. This monitoring and providing feedback is a critical part of my instruction. Using individual whiteboards allows me to easily see student responses and provides an easy way for students to correct mistakes, but you don't have to do it this way. Using paper works just fine and allows you to track their progress over time.

BEHIND THE SCENES

Spiraling Review

In addition to focusing on the new skill in the lesson, I fold in words from previous lessons to review.

TRANSITION TIP

Play the Eraser Game

I use the Eraser Game (Reading Horizons, 2019) to transition from word dictation to sentence dictation. Students have anywhere from 5–10 words written on their boards. I give a clue for each word. It might be related to meaning or phonics skill. For example, after writing several *ch* words, I might say, "Point to the word that means to cut something. I might do this to carrots before I put them in soup. What word?" (*chop*) "Yes, erase the word *chop*." Then I might say, "Point to the word with the sound /u/ in the middle. What word?" (*such*). "Yes, erase the word *such*." I would continue until all the words were erased. Then our boards are erased and we're ready to move into sentence dictation.

I choose one student who has written the word correctly (and neatly) to write it on the board for the whole class. The student will often explain how they tackled the word—for example, they might share why they used *-ck* at the end of the word (because it comes after a short vowel) or why they included an *e* at the end (so the other vowel spells its long sound). I find doing this elevates the quality of responses because all the children want to be selected next to go to the board! They love getting to write and explain the word, just like a teacher. This also allows me more time to monitor and help students.

6 SENTENCE DICTATION

Whole class, at desks, 4–5 minutes

After word dictation, comes sentence dictation. I say a sentence to students, have them repeat it, we count the number of words in it, and they write it. Here's an example:

1. I say, "The sentence is: The dog ran up the hill."
2. Students repeat, "The dog ran up the hill."
3. I say, "Let's count the words. Ready? The | dog | ran | up | the | hill." (We put a finger up for each word)
4. I say, "Now say the sounds as you write the words in the sentence."

Again, I walk around the room to monitor students and provide immediate feedback. I repeat the sentence for students who need help remembering it. As students finish, they raise their hands for me to check their sentence. Once I have looked at it to ensure accuracy, they can illustrate the sentence. They love this part, and it motivates them to complete the sentence. When everyone is done, we chorally read the sentence and then students share their pictures with a neighbor.

BEHIND THE SCENES

Weaving in Handwriting

I have students use dry-erase boards with handwriting lines so they can attend to proper letter formation and spacing during our phonics lessons.

TRANSITION TIP

Move From Sentence Dictation to High-Frequency Word Instruction

At the end of sentence dictation, when students are enthusiastically sharing their pictures with a neighbor, I say, "Eyes back on me in 3-2-1-0" to regain their attention. If I don't have everyone's attention by 0, then I get a point on the T/S Point game. Then I remind students of my expectations when I get to 0, and tell them we'll practice again. I ask them to turn and chat with their neighbor. As soon as they start chatting, I say, "Eyes back on me in 3-2-1-0." If everyone is ready by 0, I give them a point. Once everyone has refocused, I move on to high-frequency word instruction.

7 HIGH-FREQUENCY WORD INSTRUCTION

Whole class, at desks, 5 minutes

I use this opportunity to fit in my high-frequency word instruction since we already have our dry-erase boards out. Sometimes I do this step in between word and sentence dictation, especially when I include the word in our dictated sentence. A high-frequency word is a word that occurs often in text. While some high-frequency words have reliable sound-spelling correspondences (e.g., *can, it*), others include spellings that are irregular for students either because they haven't been taught yet (e.g., *her, saw*) or because they are permanently irregular (e.g., *said, of*). These irregular words require more practice for students to learn them. I often call these words "heart words" to emphasize that there is a part in the word we have to learn by heart. Here's the routine, based on the work of Nora Chahbazi and the EBLI program.

1. Say the word (e.g., *they*) and use it in a sentence to give it meaning and context.

   "The heart word we will learn today is *they*. What word? (*they*). They are going to the park."

2. Segment and count the sounds.

   "Tell me the sounds you hear in the word *they*. (/th/ /ay/). How many sounds? (2). That's right. Let's say the sounds again while we write the sound lines. /th/ /ay/."

   Students create lines on their whiteboard for each sound.

3. Map the phonemes (sounds) to the graphemes (spellings).

   "What's the first sound? (/th/) Yes. Say /th/ as you write *t-h* on the first line."

   Students write *th* on the first line.

   "What's the next sound? (/ay/). Yes. Watch carefully. In this word, the sound /ay/ is spelled with *e-y*. Write *e-y* on the next line."

   Students write *ey* on the last line.

4. Point out the irregular parts.

   "Which spelling is unusual or tricky? (*ey*). Yes, *e-y* is an unusual spelling for the sound /ay/. Let's circle that part and put two lines under it since two letters spell that sound."

5. Cover the word and have students rewrite it from memory.

   "Erase the letters, but leave the lines and circles to help you remember where the unusual part goes. Now rewrite the word and see if you can remember the spellings."

6. Uncover the word and check students' spelling.

   Show students the correct spelling, then check their work and, if necessary, correct their spellings.

7. Have students generate sentences that contain the word.

   Students orally compose a sentence with the word and share it with their neighbor.

TRANSITION TIP

Move From High-Frequency Word Instruction to Partner Word Reading

To transition from high-frequency word instruction to partner word reading, I ask students to erase their boards and put them away while I pass out the word lists. I might count back from five to keep them moving. As soon as they get the word list, they begin reading with their partners.

8 PARTNER WORD READING

Whole class in pairs, at desks, 2–3 minutes

I pass out lists of words containing the targeted skill for students to read with a partner. Partner 1 reads the word list while Partner 2 follows along, and then they switch. They continue taking turns until I say stop.

TRANSITION TIP

Move From Reading Words to Reading Texts

I check in to help a few students as they read their word lists and then begin passing out the decodable passage while they continue reading. After a few minutes of word reading, we can move directly into the decodable passage routine since the passages have already been passed out.

9 DECODABLE TEXT READING

Whole class, at desks, 10 minutes

Students need plenty of opportunities to practice the phoneme-grapheme correspondences you are teaching them by reading connected text. It would be a mistake to practice those skills only in isolation. Making a decodable-text routine part of your phonics lesson ensures students have the chance to apply new learning.

> **BEHIND THE SCENES**
> **Highlighting Books**
> My district adopted a new phonics curriculum this year that comes with a class set of decodable books. We're not allowed to highlight in those books, so I skip Steps 2 and 3.

1. Give each student a copy of the decodable text.
2. Give them 1–2 minutes to highlight the targeted skill words in the text.
3. Have students read the highlighted words as a class, individually, or with a partner.
4. Choral-read or partner-read the passage (or do both if you have time).
   - **Choral-read routine:** Model the first paragraph, and then have students chorally read the first paragraph. Model the second paragraph, and then have students chorally read the second paragraph, etc.
   - **Partner-read routine:** Have Partner 1 read the first paragraph, and then have Partner 2 read the first paragraph. Have Partner 1 read the second paragraph, and then have Partner 2 read the second paragraph, etc.
5. Ask questions about the passage or have students retell it to a partner.
6. If time permits, give students a few minutes to illustrate the passage.

Variation: Have students whisper-read the text independently. You might build this in before you choral-read or after students partner-read.

We end the lesson where we began: on the rug, which helps everyone listen attentively as we review key points. I love the close-knit feeling that being on the rug brings.

Partner reading with decodable texts allows students to apply the phoneme-grapheme correspondences they're learning.

10 CLOSE

Whole class, on the rug, 1–2 minutes

At this point, I offer a brief review of the critical content that I taught, give students some retrieval practice, and preview what they will learn in the next lesson.

The physical location(s) of and transitions in your phonics lesson might be different from mine, and that's okay! I offer these details as simply an example. Your students, classroom setup, furniture, technology, etc., all come into play here. You need to decide what works best for you, your classroom, your students, and the flow of your instruction.

TRANSITION TIP

Clean Up

When students finish reading and discussing the decodable text, they rise from their chairs, push them in, and stand with their text and word list in hand. I excuse one row at a time to put materials in cubbies to take home. Then students return to the rug for our lesson closing.

Remember, smooth transitions free up valuable time for learning. Having a well-structured flow keeps students engaged in the learning and minimizes disruption.

Schedule Considerations: Finding Your Groove

Fitting everything in is always a challenge! I don't always have time for all the parts of the lesson, especially at the beginning of the year when we are still learning our routines. It also depends on whether I have 30 or 45 minutes available for my phonics lesson. Here's how I prioritize:

- Phonemic Awareness Warm-Up: I do this every day.
- Review: I aim to do the three-part drill at least three times per week.
- New Concept Introduction: Typically, I dedicate two days on a concept. So on the second day, this part of the lesson is a brief reminder.
- Choral Word Reading: I do this every day.
- Word Dictation: I do this every day, sometimes substituting in a word chain or word sort on the second day of the concept.
- Sentence Dictation: I do this on the second day of the concept.
- High-Frequency Word Instruction: I prefer teaching only a few words a week, so I might not introduce a new one every lesson. I review them each day, though.
- Partner Word Reading: I do this every day.
- Decodable Text Reading: I target whole-class decodable text reading at least three times a week. If I have 45 minutes for my phonics lesson, I include decodable text reading in every lesson.
- Close: I do this every day.

Given that, here's how my weekly schedule might look for 30-minute lessons:

Monday	Tuesday	Wednesday	Thursday	Friday
Phonemic Awareness Warm-Up 2 minutes	**Phonemic Awareness Warm-Up** 1 minute	**Phonemic Awareness Warm-Up** 1 minute	**Phonemic Awareness Warm-Up** 2 minutes	**Phonemic Awareness Warm-Up** 1 minute
Review-3 Part Drill 5 minutes		**Review-3 Part Drill** 5 minutes		**Review-3 Part Drill** 4 minutes
New Concept Introduction 3 minutes	**New Concept Review** 3 minutes	**New Concept Introduction** 1 minute	**New Concept Review** 1 minute	**New Concept Introduction** 2 minutes
Choral Word Reading 2 minutes	**Choral Word Reading** 2 minutes	**Choral Word Reading** 2 minutes	**Choral Word Reading** 2 minutes	**Choral Word Reading** 1 minute
Word Dictation 10 minutes	**Word Dictation** 8 minutes	**Word Dictation** 10 minutes	**Word Dictation** 5 minutes	**Word Dictation** 9 minutes
High- Frequency Word Instruction 5 minutes	**Sentence Dictation** 5 minutes	**High-Frequency Word Instruction** 5 minutes	**Sentence Dictation** 5 minutes	
Partner Word Reading 3 minutes	**Partner Word Reading** 3 minutes	**Partner Word Reading** 2 minutes	**Partner Word Reading** 2 minutes	**Partner Word Reading** 2 minutes
	Decodable Text 12 minutes		**Decodable Text** 12 minutes	**Decodable Text** 10 minutes
Close 2 minutes	**Close** 2 minutes	**Close** 1 minute	**Close** 1 minute	**Close** 1 minute

In Closing, Remember...

There are many things to consider as you plan your daily phonics lesson. Take time to think about physical location(s) of and transitions between parts. Think about your seating arrangements and assignments, whether your students are on the rug or at their desks. Do you have routines in place? Is there room for improvement? How can you tighten up transitions? Is there anything you can do to maximize the learning time and reduce the transition time? Look over your lesson steps, consider the physical layout of your classroom, and decide how students will move and transition between activities. Additionally, improve the delivery of your lesson by maintaining a quick pace, eliciting frequent responses, monitoring carefully, and providing immediate feedback.

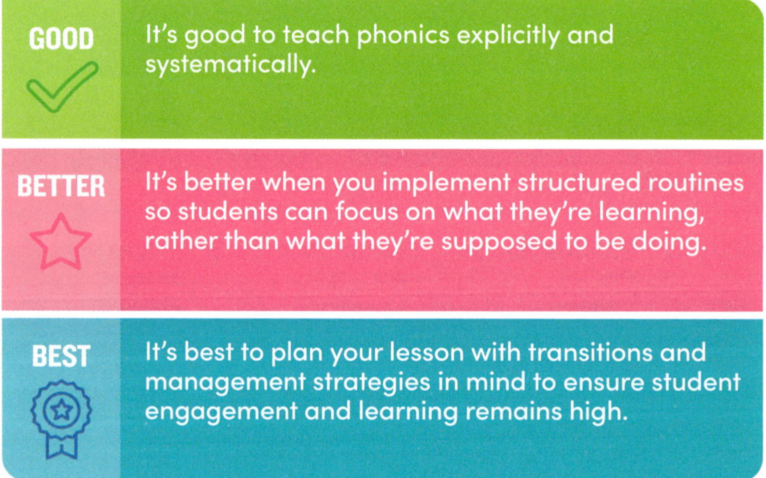

Opening Act: Close Reading

CHAPTER 4

SPOTLIGHT ON CLOSE READING

I start the close reading lesson by introducing some vocabulary words and building background knowledge that is critical to understanding the text we will read. Next, I read the text aloud while students follow along in their own copies of the text, or students choral-read it with me, or they read it on their own, with a partner. Regardless of how students experience the text, I pause to discuss important ideas, ask questions, or explain any difficult words or concepts. After reading, we discuss the text and generate a gist, or main idea, statement.

DOMINANT MOVES FROM *7 MIGHTY MOVES*

MOVE 6: Focus on Meaningful Fluency Practice

MOVE 7: Improve Comprehension by Developing Vocabulary and Background Knowledge

My goals for close reading are to target vocabulary, build knowledge, develop reading fluency, and, ultimately, deepen comprehension of a complex text that I've carefully chosen. The text is at the center and my lesson steps are built around it.

> **Lindsay Live!** Enter her classroom to learn more about writing.
>
> 

That doesn't mean I don't spend any time teaching my students comprehension strategies (such as identifying main idea and summarizing the text). I certainly do, but not in isolation, for example, by focusing on a new strategy each week. Now that I've really dug into the science of reading, I realize there's much more to it. Instead, again, I center my instruction around the text, rather than the strategy. Teaching a strategy is not an end in itself, but rather a means to an end: for my students to gain knowledge while they read. When students apply strategies to new texts, they gain even more knowledge.

Close-Reading Lesson Steps

1. Before Reading

- Teach Pronunciation of Unfamiliar Words
- Teach/Review Vocabulary
- Teach/Activate Critical Background Knowledge

2. During Reading

Options:

- Teacher Reads the Text
- Choral-Read
- Partner-Read

3. After Reading

Options:

- Paragraph Shrinking/Finding the Gist
- Ask Questions to Engage in Discussion
- Generate Questions
- Determine Text Structure
- Summarize or Retell the Text
- Vocabulary Application
- Fluency Practice
- Written Response

I use authentic, complex texts for close reading. Complex texts are texts that are challenging for students to read and understand. They may be above grade level or, though at grade level, require supportive instruction to ensure understanding. It's important for students to be exposed to many different types of texts, not just decodable texts, but I don't expect them to read these complex texts on their own until they're ready.

Reading aloud during close reading is a wonderful way for students to hear advanced language, vocabulary, and content. It provides an opportunity to work on the language-comprehension strands of the Reading Rope (Scarborough, 2001).

In addition to reading aloud to students, it's important to scaffold them into reading complex texts themselves when they are ready. Close reading is when I get to help facilitate this by engaging students in echo-, choral-, and partner-reading. It's exhilarating to see students start to apply their phonics knowledge to new words.

Does your reading program contain complex texts? If not, create text sets that feature a focus text and several support texts on a similar topic. These support texts should prepare students to read the focus text by building relevant background knowledge or deepen their understanding of the focus text after reading.

A Closer Look at Each Step

Let's take a closer look at the lesson by focusing on what I do before, during, and after reading the text with my students.

The steps I take before reading can differ slightly depending on whether the students or I are reading the text. Remember, the close-reading lesson is an opportunity to focus on the language-comprehension strands of the Reading Rope. Because of that, I often read the text aloud to students so they can experience it without the added pressure of decoding the words, especially when the text is well above grade level. Other times, I want students to read the text themselves, especially as their decoding abilities improve. In that case, I prepare them by teaching the pronunciation of any unfamiliar words that will appear in the text.

1 BEFORE READING

Whole class, on the rug or at desks, 5–10 minutes

- Teach Pronunciation of Unfamiliar Words (if students are reading the text)
- Teach/Review Vocabulary
- Teach/Activate Critical Background Knowledge

I usually start our close-reading lessons on the rug, but the location can change depending on our initial activities. I love the more focused, united feel on the rug, but I might choose to start the lesson at our desks.

Teach Pronunciation of Unfamiliar Words (If students will read the text)

1–3 minutes

To prepare students to read the text, I briefly review 2–5 words they may have trouble reading–usually irregular high-frequency words (such as *though* and *laugh*) and/or content-related words (such as *pyramids* and *ocean*). I write the words on the board before the lesson and then review them with students at the start of the lesson. I skip this step if I'm reading the text aloud to students.

1. I say, "Here are some words you'll see in our story today. This is the word *caught*. He *caught* the ball.

   What word?" (*caught*)

2. "Yes, tell me the sounds in *caught*."
3. "That's right. As you look at this word, show me on your fingers how many letters you think spell the /au/ sound."
4. "Yes, there are 4 letters: *augh* spell the /au/ sound in this word. Let's sound it out and read the word again."
5. "Here's another word in our story. We've learned this word before, but some of us are still learning it. This is the word, "*are*." What word? (*are*). Yes. We *are* going to read an interesting story."
6. I point back up at the first word, "What word?" (*caught*). I point at the next word, "What word?" (*are*).
7. Repeat similarly for the remaining words.

Teach/Review Vocabulary

3–8 minutes

Some vocabulary words require only a quick explanation and others require the full instructional routine. I normally teach between 3–5 words per text. If we spend more than one day on a text, I spend more time on vocabulary instruction on the first day and give quick reviews on the remaining days that include opportunities to interact with and practice using the word. My routine comes from Archer and Hughes's wonderful book, *Explicit Instruction: Effective and Efficient Teaching* (2010).

1. Introduce the word and its pronunciation.

   Display the word and have students repeat it. Clap or pound the syllables of the word.

Using actions helps students grasp the meanings of our vocabulary words.

2. Give a simple, student-friendly definition.

   Dictionary definitions are often more confusing than the word itself! I use the *Longman Dictionary of Contemporary English Online* to find easy-to-understand definitions. Avoid asking if students know what the word means, because you might get an incorrect answer that causes confusion and that the other students tend to remember.

3. Illustrate the word with examples.

   Consider acting it out or use a gesture, show a picture, or explain it verbally.

4. Check students' understanding.

   Have students identify examples and non-examples, or ask a question related to the words' meaning.

BEHIND THE SCENES

Using Vocabulary Cards

My vocabulary cards have words written on them, along with illustrations to match. After introducing the words, I place the cards in a pocket chart to remind us to interact with and review them throughout the week.

TRANSITION TIP

Prepare Materials

Transitions are pretty simple so far because students remain in one spot. Again, my preparation makes all the difference. Before students arrive, I set out the text we are going to read, vocabulary cards, my teacher manual, and any needed visuals, and place them on the shelf behind my whiteboard easel so everything is in easy reach.

BEHIND THE SCENES

Building Knowledge

You don't need to teach everything about the topic for students to understand the text. They will build knowledge as you read the text and discuss it.

TRANSITION TIP

Keep a Quick Pace

Pacing is everything! I keep a quick pace to ensure we have time for reading and discussing the text.

Repeat with the remaining words. Depending on the amount of time I have, I might break up the routine. I might teach Steps 1–3, and save Step 4 for another time or day.

Teach/Activate Critical Background Knowledge

1–5 minutes

We'll be building knowledge as we read the text, but if there is anything necessary to teach beforehand, I address it before the reading. I find these four steps helpful (Stevens & Austin, 2022; Vaughn et al., 2013):

1. Summarize the big idea of the unit we are in.
2. Connect the new learning with prior learning.
3. Use a visual to support important information (e.g., picture, object, map, video clip).
4. Ask a comprehension question to give a purpose for reading the text.

   Here's an example:

   - I say, "We are learning all about the people in ancient Asia."
   - I continue, "Yesterday we learned that rivers were important to these people. Why were the rivers important?" (Pause for think time, a turn-and-talk, then have a couple students share.) "In our story today, we are going to learn about something else that was important to the people: writing. Why is writing important to us today?" (Answers vary.)
   - I show a picture and say, "Look at this picture of some ancient writing. This is called *cuneiform*. Say that. (*cuneiform*) The people would write these symbols on clay tablets."
   - I set a purpose by saying, "Let's read the story to find out more about this type of writing and why it was important."

2 DURING READING

Whole class, at desks, 12–20 minutes

Options:

- Teacher Reads the Text
- Choral-Read
- Partner-Read

Now comes the best part: reading the text! As we read the text, I pause periodically to explain something, think aloud, model a strategy (such as summarization or self-monitoring), or ask a question. I might think aloud the process I'm using to understand the text. I might start by saying, "I'm confused here because..." or "I wonder if...." or "Now I understand that..." When I ask questions, I often ask students to turn and talk to discuss possible answers with a neighbor before we discuss the question and possible answers all together.

TRANSITION TIP

Smooth the Transition to Desks

After the Before Reading activities, I say, "desk, desk, desk." Students repeat "desk, desk, desk," and move swiftly to their desks. As they are transitioning, I pass out the books or passages. If they move quickly and quietly, they earn a point on the T/S chart.

Think-Aloud Prompts

Use the following prompts from Ness and Kenny (2015) as you think aloud for your students:

- I wonder...
- I predict...
- I don't understand...
- This reminds me of...
- When I read this, I think...
- This does not make sense to me because...
- I already know something about...
- I think I will learn...
- I wonder what it means when...
- I can picture...
- I think...because it said...
- The most important thing I have learned so far is...
- It was interesting to me because...
- I really like how the author...
- I think/I bet...
- Now that I reread, I...
- I am confused by this...
- This reminds me of...

(Ness & Kenny, 2015)

TRANSITION TIP

Regain Students' Attention

Turn and talks are terrific, but you can lose instructional time trying to regain students' attention. To get their eyes back on me, I count back from three. If, by the time I get to zero, they are quiet and ready to listen, I give them a point on the T/S chart; if they are not, I get the point or I might have them practice again (or both). I keep my expectations high, and students rise to the occasion, and we make the most of the precious instructional minutes we have.

BEHIND THE SCENES

Avoiding Tangents

Keep yourself and your students focused on the text. Don't get sidetracked by unrelated stories or comments.

The way we read the text depends on several things, such as how difficult the text is and the abilities of my students. I use a combination of read-aloud, choral-reading, and partner-reading. If the text is well above grade level, I read it aloud to students. If the text is at or slightly above grade level, I might begin by reading it aloud to model accurate, fluent reading and prepare students to read the text themselves. Next, I'll have students practice the text through choral-reading or partner-reading. It's all about scaffolding students as they tackle a complex text. The most supportive practice is reading it aloud to them, followed by choral-reading and, finally, partner-reading. Sometimes I spread readings across days, and sometimes I do them all in one day! One thing remains constant: students consume the text and I ask questions along the way to help them build an understanding of the text. Let me describe one way I might do this:

Day 1: Teacher Reads the Text

After our "Before Reading" instruction, I read aloud the text to students. This text might be the same one students will read on Day 2, or it might be a support text designed to build background knowledge in preparation for the reading on Day 2. I pause occasionally to explain or think aloud about a point or ask a question. Then I move to one of the "After Reading" activities (see below).

Day 2: Choral-Read

After our "Before Reading" activities (teaching unfamiliar and vocabulary words), I direct students to their desks and pass out copies of the text. I read a page or paragraph to students, modeling appropriate rate, phrasing, and expression, while students follow along with a finger to stay engaged. Then students choral-read the *same* page or paragraph. Then I read a second page or paragraph, and students choral-read the same page or paragraph. We continue reading like this for the rest of the text. If time allows, we read the text again, but this time with a partner. If not, we move into one of the After Reading activities.

While students read the text with a partner, I circulate the room providing feedback and support as needed.

Day 3: Partner-Read

After reviewing unfamiliar and vocabulary words (our Before Reading activities), students read the same text we read on Day 2 with a partner in the same way they choral-read it with me on Day 2. Partner 1 reads page or paragraph 1, then Partner 2 reads page or paragraph 1; Partner 1 reads page or paragraph 2, then Partner 2 reads page or paragraph 2; and so on. I walk around to assist and manage students as needed.

*** Kindergarten Note:** I will use read-alouds for the close-reading portion of the day the entire year. If I implement any kind of partner-reading or choral-reading, it is part of my phonics instruction with decodable text.

*** First-Grade Note:** Most first graders are not ready to partner-read complex text until the middle of the year. While I might do some limited choral-reading the first half of the year, especially when the text is simple, I don't expect my students to read this text independently or with a partner until January or February, when they have a solid grasp of phonics and are starting to transition away from decodable texts.

TRANSITION TIP

Assign Seats Wisely

I assign students to sit next to their reading partner to help our transition to partner-reading flow better. Sometimes I need to move students due to personalities and work habits. In this case, those students know to change seats quickly in preparation for reading with their partner.

BEHIND THE SCENES
Assigning Partners

I am intentional when I pair students for partner-reading. I list my students from least fluent to most fluent and then divide the list in half. I pair the least fluent student in one half, with the least fluent in the other half, the next-least fluent in one half, with the next-least fluent in the other half, and so on. I assign the stronger reader in each pair Reader 1 or the "milk," and I assign the weaker reader in each pair Reader 2 or the "cookie." Of course, I do not tell students who the stronger/weaker readers are... they just know whether they are the milk or the cookie, and that the milks read first. This means weaker students have more modeling and support when it's their time to read.

3 AFTER READING

Whole class, on the rug or at desks, 5–15 minutes

Options:

- Paragraph Shrinking/Finding the Gist
- Ask Questions to Engage in Discussion
- Generate Questions
- Determine Text Structure
- Summarize or Retell Text
- Vocabulary Application
- Fluency Practice
- Written Response

There are a lot of options for what we do after reading a text. I prioritize identifying the main idea (Paragraph Shrinking/Finding the Gist) because it is critical to understanding any text (Shanahan, 2005). From there, I choose an activity based on available time, the text complexity, and what will be most helpful for my students.

Paragraph Shrinking/Finding the Gist

Identifying a text's main idea is an important skill to have, but it can also be challenging for students. Rather than just asking students to find the main idea, we need to teach them *how* to find it. Paragraph Shrinking (Fuchs et al., 2008) or Finding the Gist (Klingner et al., 1998) are similar ways to help students do that. My students engage in those activities with almost every text we close read. This is also where I build in sentence-level instruction in grammar and syntax. I can also show students how to expand their main idea statements into summaries of the text.

1. Ask students, "What is the most important *who* or *what* this story is about?" Write responses on the whiteboard.
2. Ask, "What's the most important thing about the *who* or *what*?" or "What did the character do?" Discuss possible answers and write one on the board.
3. Combine the two responses into one sentence, or gist statement, as a model. Then have students turn to a partner to verbally craft another way to construct a sentence.
4. Call on a few students to share their sentences.
5. If time allows, have students write their gist statements in notebooks independently or as a shared writing activity, or write a statement yourself with input from the students.

I start the year with modeling and assigning a "who" and "do" for our gist statement. As the school year goes on, I show students how to add other details and craft more advanced sentences, by adding in a "when," "where," and "how" or "why" (Jennings & Haynes 2018; Laud & Patel, 2023). Students enjoy coming up with ways to combine that information in a well-written sentence. See the next page for ways my first graders constructed sentences after reading a text about Thomas Edison.

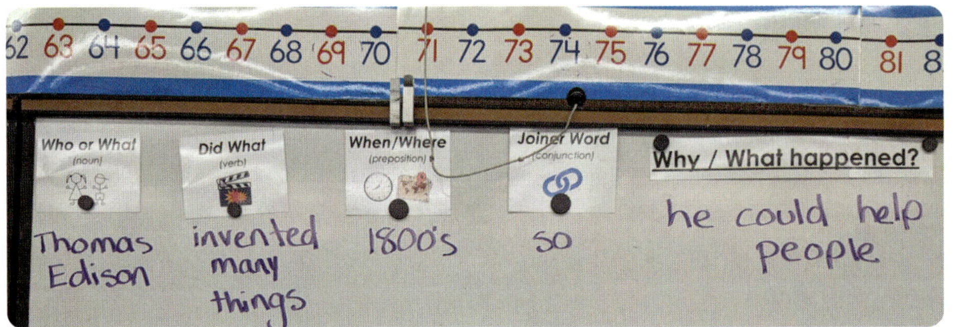

Download illustrated cards to use for the different parts of the gist sentence.

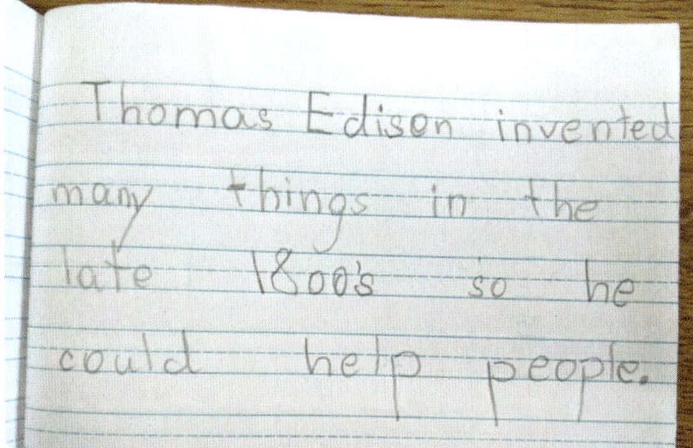

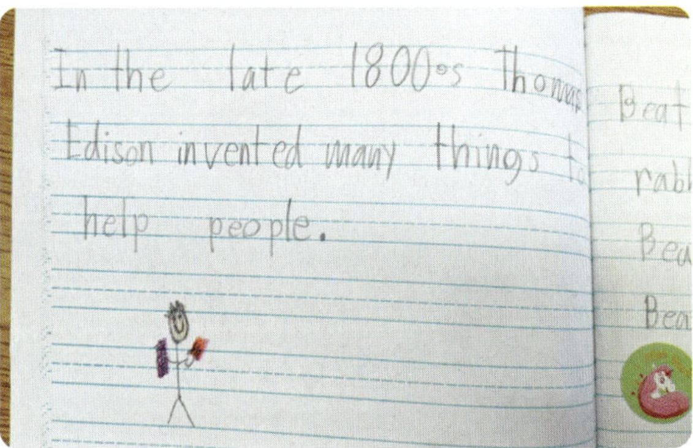

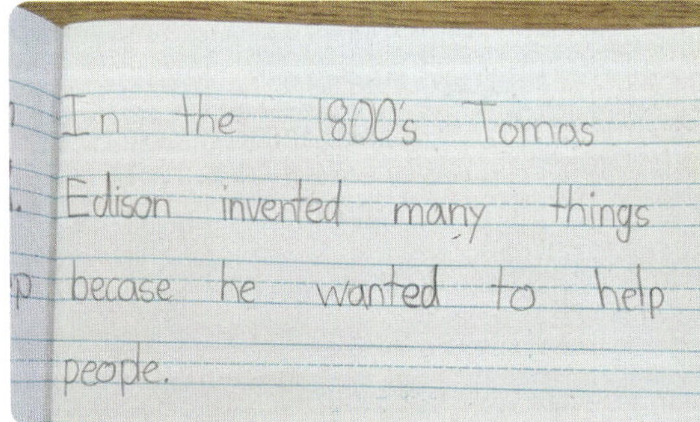

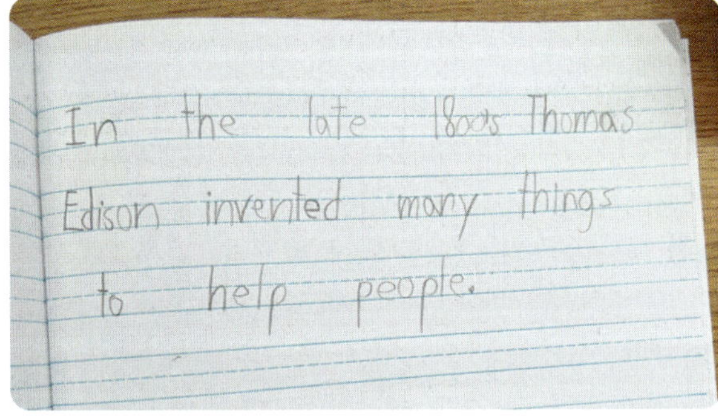

Here are some of the gist statements my first graders wrote after we read a story about Thomas Edison.

Ask Questions to Engage in Discussion

When we've finished reading the text, I ask an open-ended question about it and give students "think time" before turning to talk to a neighbor about a response. Then we come back together and discuss thoughts as a group.

Initially, I ask questions that help students understand the text structure, such as, "Was there a problem? Why was it happening? Was it solved? How?" Then, I ask deeper questions that require inferencing, such as, "What lesson do you think Little Red Riding Hood learned?" I often provide a sentence stem to ensure students speak in complete sentences. For example, I might say "Start with, 'I think Little Red Riding Hood learned...'"

BEHIND THE SCENES

Prepping Questions

Our discussions always go better when I've read and pondered the text beforehand. I appreciate when my core program provides thought-provoking questions about the text, allowing me more time to plan for other parts of the day. If it doesn't, I devote time before school to prepare questions.

Generate Questions

When students generate questions about a text on their own and answer them, they process that text more actively (National Reading Panel, 2000).

1. Say, "Now, you get to be the teacher and come up with a question you might ask about the text."

   "Who can think of a *where* question about this book?"

2. After allowing them time to think and come up with questions on their own, say "Cookies, ask your *where* question to your neighbor. Milks, answer their question. Then switch and Milks ask your question and Cookies answer."

3. Repeat process with another question (*who*, *what*, *when*, *why*, or *how*).

BEHIND THE SCENES

Scaffolding Questions

Coming up with questions can be hard for students. So you might scaffold it by rereading a paragraph from the text and helping students create a question about that specific part of the text. If students continue to struggle, scaffold further by rereading just one sentence and showing them how to flip it into a question.

BEHIND THE SCENES

Identifying Partners

To promote balanced participation, pair up students and give each one a unique identifier, such as Partner 1 and Partner 2, A and B, milk and cookie. This will help you target directions (e.g., "Partner 1s, think about your answer before giving it to Partner 2") and encourage both students to contribute equally.

Determine Text Structure

Teach text structure explicitly to improve students' comprehension and take their main idea statements even further. With the Knowledge Acquisition and Transformation (KAT) Framework (Hudson et al., 2021; Wijekumar et al., 2023), the teacher hints at a text's structure before reading the text, and then invites students to think about how the author organized the text, during and after reading, focusing on one of three structures: comparison, cause and effect, and problem and solution. She urges students to focus on the text's signal words to help them identify the structure.

After reading, the teacher leads a conversation with students about the structure. Then she has students use sentence stems based on the overall structure (see table below) to create a more detailed main idea statement, followed by a summary. Here's an example:

1. I say, "Remember, authors choose certain text structures to organize their ideas. When we figure out the structure, we can better understand the text."
2. "As I read the story closely, I noticed some words that gave me a hint about what the structure might be: *trouble*, *difficulty*, and *risk*."
3. "Was there a problem in this story?" (Discuss.)
4. "Was there a solution?" (If there is not a solution, it's a cause-and-effect structure; if there is a solution, it's a problem-and-solution structure.)
5. "I think this text must be a problem-and-solution structure. Let's make a statement together. The main problem is ________, and the main solution is _________. Wonderful."
6. "We can add more details to our statement to summarize the text. Listen as I try it." (Model for students.) "Now it's your turn. Turn to your neighbor and summarize the story by adding details to the sentence we wrote."

   The evidence behind the KAT framework is impressive. You can learn more about it at the literacy.IO website.

Main Idea and Summary Quick Guide

	Comparison	Cause and Effect	Problem and Solution
Signaling Words (not exclusive)	instead, but, however, or alternatively, whereas, on the other hand, while, compare, in comparison, in contrast, resemble, the same as, all but, have in common, similarities, differentiate, options, less than, act like, look like, just as, more than, longer than, despite, although, just, difference, different	cause, lead to, bring about, originate, produce, make possible, by, since, due to, because, in order to, reasons, give reasons for, the reason why, on account of, in explanation, effect, affects, so, influenced by, as a result, result from, consequence, consequent, thus, therefore	problem, trouble, difficulty, hazard, need to prevent, threat, danger, puzzle, issue, risk, to satisfy the problem, ways to reduce the problem, to solve these problems, protection from the problem, solution, response, answer, reply, comeback, recommendation, return, suggestions
Main Idea Stem	________ and ________ were compared on ________, ________, and ________.	The main cause is ________ and the main effect is ________.	The cause of the problem is ________. The main problem is ________, and the main solution is ________.
Recall/Summary Stem	The first topic of comparison is ________. [The topic] is/has [state what was learned about the topic for that specific comparison category]. In contrast (or another signaling word), the second idea is ________. [The topic] is/has [state what was, learned about the topic].	The cause was ________ [state what was learned about the cause]. The effect of this cause was ________ [state what was learned about the effect]. [Repeat for each cause/effect.]	The problem was ________ [state a description of the problem and, if known, its cause(s)]. The solution was ________ [state a description of the solution and how it gets rid of the causes(s) of the problem(s) or tries to. [Repeat for each problem and solution.]

(From Wijekumar et al., 2023, *The Reading League Journal*)

Summarize or Retell Text

After helping students construct a mental model of the text by determining the text structure, have them summarize or retell the text. Here's an example of how I do that for a narrative text. We use a story map called C-SPACE (MacArthur et al., 1991) to list the story elements. After reading the story, I record students' responses on the C-SPACE chart. Then we are ready to summarize or retell the story.

1. Say, "We can use our C-SPACE map to retell the story. Listen." Model how to retell the story referencing the story map we constructed.
2. Say, "Your turn. Turn to your neighbor. Milks, practice retelling the story to your partners while Cookies listen. Then switch."
3. Walk around to listen and provide support as needed.

Using puppets is another fun, engaging way for students to retell a story. We either use commercial puppets or I print some for students to color and cut out. It's a great way to improve oral language while reinforcing the story's key events.

Vocabulary Application

After reading is a great time to apply new vocabulary from the text. I might also check students' vocabulary knowledge with examples and non-examples of words, if I didn't have time for that step before reading. Or I might engage students in three-column notes, vocabulary skits, shades of meaning, or Word Masters to Movie Scripts. (See *7 Mighty Moves* and *7 Mighty Moves Reading Resources* for details.)

Fluency Practice

Giving students extra time after close reading to read aloud the text is a great way to provide fluency practice. Learn more about the many ways to read with a partner in *7 Mighty Moves.*

Written Response

After writing our gist statement, we might create a keyword outline and paragraph based on the text. (See *7 Mighty Moves*, page 137.) Or I might write two sentences from the text on the board for us to practice sentence combining. Or we might write in response to a prompt related to the text... which brings us to the next chapter.

Schedule Considerations: Finding Your Groove

I plan my close-reading lessons by thinking about what I'll do before, during, and after reading the text. How this part of the literacy block looks depends on the grade level and abilities of my students, the core language program I'm using, and the time of year. Remember, I'm using authentic, complex texts during this time and a combination of read-aloud, choral-reading, and partner-reading. Here's how close reading might look across the year at different grade-levels.

✱ Kindergarten Note: I read aloud all texts for close-reading lessons.

✱ First-Grade Note: At the beginning of the year, I read aloud all the texts to the students. Gradually, I mix in some echo-reading and choral-reading. By the middle of the year, I add partner-reading to the mix. So throughout the week, my students and I engage in some combination of read-alouds, choral-reading with modeling, and partner-reading. Most students are still reading decodable texts during small-group instruction, so they receive practice in authentic, complex texts and decodable texts in the second half of the year.

✱ Second-Grade Note: Students receive a mixture of read-aloud, choral-reading with modeling, and partner-reading the entire year, using authentic, complex texts.

Vocabulary instruction looks different across the week as well. If my core program includes 5–10 vocabulary words a week, I spend more time introducing those words on Monday and Tuesday, and less time on the remaining days, enough to allow brief interactions with the words for review.

Here's how a weekly schedule might look if I have 30 minutes a day for close reading. If I have less than that, I shorten the "after-reading" activities and move into our writing lesson. Ideally, the texts I use throughout the week are connected by topic.

Monday	Tuesday	Wednesday	Thursday	Friday
New Text	Same Text as Monday	New Text With Same Vocabulary Words	Same Text as Wednesday	New Text
Before Reading 8 minutes	**Before Reading** 5 minutes	**Before Reading** 4 minutes	**Before Reading** 5 minutes	**Before Reading** 4 minutes
Vocabulary 5 minutes	**Teach Unfamiliar Words** 3 minutes	**Vocabulary** 2 minutes	**Teach Unfamiliar Words** 2 minutes	**Vocabulary** 2 minutes
Activate Background Knowledge 3 minutes	**Vocabulary** 2 minutes	**Activate Background Knowledge** 2 minutes	**Vocabulary** 3 minutes	**Activate Background Knowledge** 2 minutes
During Reading 12 minutes	**During Reading** 20 minutes	**During Reading** 15 minutes	**During Reading** 15 minutes	**During Reading** 14 minutes
Read-Aloud With Discussion 12 minutes	**Choral/Model Reading** 10 minutes	**Choral/Model Reading and Discussion** 15 minutes	**Partner-Reading** 15 minutes	**Read-Aloud With Discussion** 8 minutes
	Partner Reading 10 minutes			**Choral-Read** 6 minutes
After Reading 10 minutes	**After Reading** 5 minutes	**After Reading** 11 minutes	**After Reading** 10 minutes	**After Reading** 12 minutes
Engage in Discussion and Gist Statement 5 minutes	**Generate and Answer Questions** 5 minutes	**Engage in Discussion; Gist Statement and Summarize** 11 minutes	**Determine Text Structure and Summarize** 5 minutes	**Engage in Discussion and Gist Statement** 5 minutes
Story Map and Retell 5 minutes			**Vocabulary Application** 5 minutes	**Generate and Answer Questions** 3 minutes
				Retell With Puppets 5 minutes

In Closing, Remember...

Remember, the close-reading lesson is an opportunity to focus on the language-comprehension strands of the Reading Rope. Center your instruction around the text, rather than the strategy, and teach strategies to help students build knowledge from and understand the text. Plan your close-reading lessons by thinking about what you'll do before, during, and after reading the text.

Dive deeper into comprehension and close reading by exploring the following resources:

Know Better, Do Better: Comprehension by David and Meredith Liben

The Reading Comprehension Blueprint by Nancy Lewis Hennessy

See the professional online course on the KAT method at the literacy.IO website

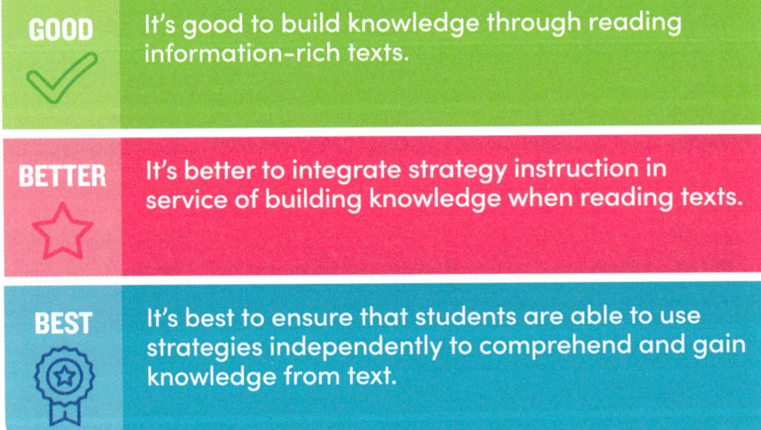

Show Time: Writing

CHAPTER 5

SPOTLIGHT ON WRITING

Our writing lesson starts off with my students and me chanting or singing the parts of the writing process. Together, we analyze the weekly writing prompt I've assigned and brainstorm how we might respond to it. Next, we pick ideas that work best to answer the prompt and organize them into an outline.

On subsequent days, we use our outlines to construct paragraphs, as a group, in pairs, or independently. When we're done, we score our writing and set a goal for what we can do better next time.

DOMINANT MOVES FROM *7 MIGHTY MOVES*

MOVE 1: Teach Phonemic Awareness With Intention

MOVE 2: Teach Phonics Explicitly and Systematically

MOVE 5: Embrace a Better Approach to Teaching "Sight Words"

MOVE 7: Improve Comprehension by Developing Vocabulary and Background Knowledge

Many of the moves I've been making for writing lately are centered around using Self-Regulated Strategy Development (SRSD), developed by Karen Harris and researched by Harris, her colleagues, and others. SRSD is an evidence-based approach to writing instruction that includes not only teaching writing strategies but also self-regulation strategies. Extensive research has shown that SRSD helps students become more effective writers (Harris et al., 2023; Kim et al., 2024), and it consistently has the highest effect sizes of all writing interventions (Graham et al., 2013; Harris, 2024). In addition to explicit teaching and modeling, students actively collaborate in SRSD through whole-class and peer discussions. The instruction emphasizes rich discussions to build academic vocabulary, concepts, and knowledge (Harris, 2024).

Lindsay Live! Enter her classroom to learn more about writing.

The goals of SRSD are to:

1. Assist students in learning strategies involved in the writing process, including planning, writing, revising, and editing.
2. Support students in monitoring and managing their own writing.
3. Foster positive attitudes toward writing and in seeing themselves as writers. (Harris et al., 2003)

Self-talk is an integral part of SRSD and one way for students to develop self-regulation strategies, such as self-assessment, self-monitoring, and self-reinforcement. It helps students manage frustration (e.g., This is so hard, but I know I can do it. I can take one step at a time), evaluate their work (e.g., Did I include all the parts of TIDE (see page 89)? Did I answer the prompt?), and develop positive attitudes about writing (e.g., I did my best. I'm an amazing writer!). I model this for students, and we brainstorm a list of statements we can say to ourselves as we write. Students often choose a favorite self-statement to write down on their paper as a reminder.

Writing Lesson Steps

(Adapted from thinkSRSD)

On Day 1:

1. Review POW
2. Review TIDE
3. Collaborative Practice: Plan and Organize
4. Orally Rehearse the Paragraph

On Subsequent Days:

5. Collaborative or Independent Practice: Write
6. Color Code and Score
7. Set Goals

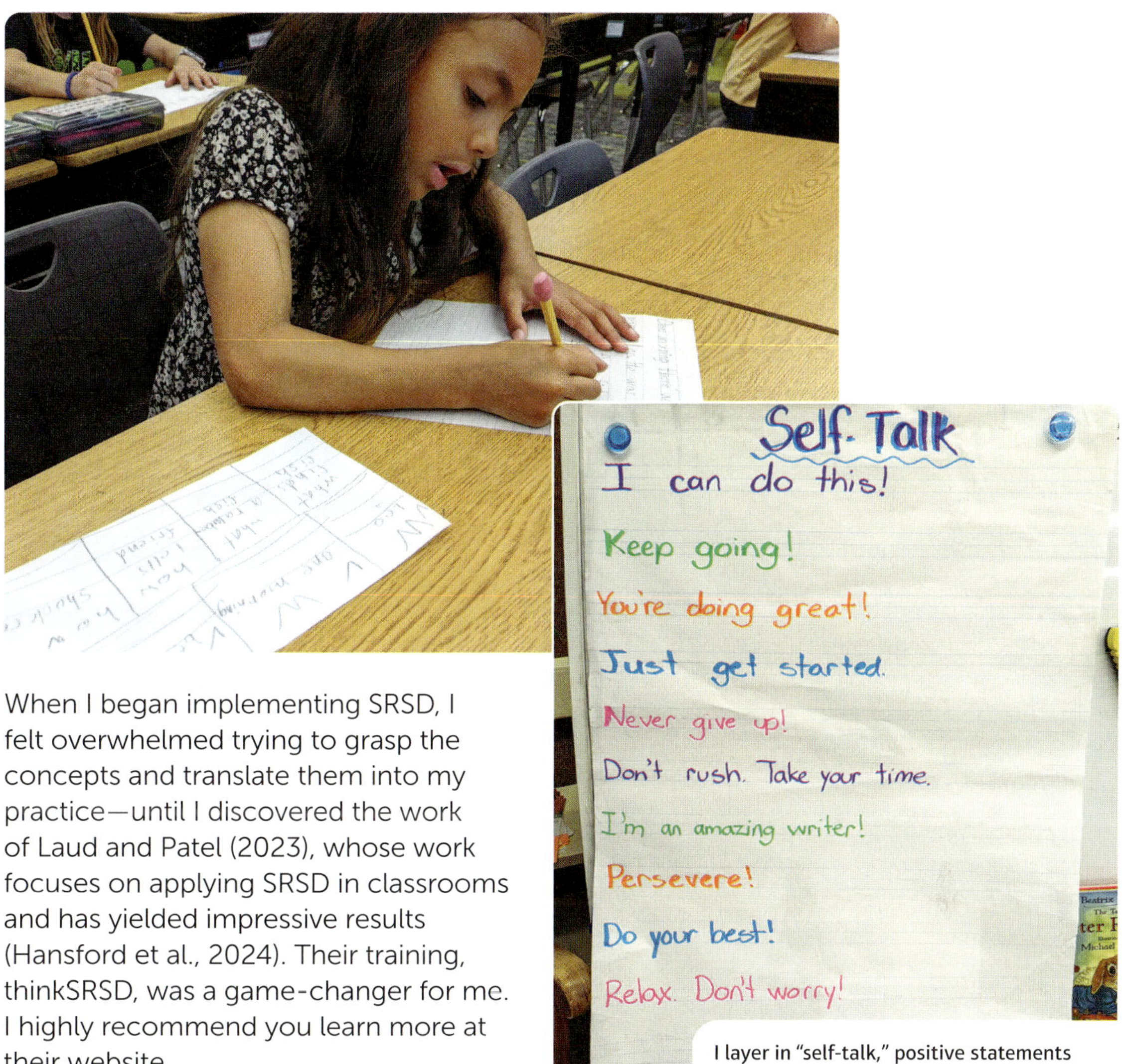

I layer in "self-talk," positive statements students can say to themselves as they write to monitor their progress and stay motivated.

When I began implementing SRSD, I felt overwhelmed trying to grasp the concepts and translate them into my practice—until I discovered the work of Laud and Patel (2023), whose work focuses on applying SRSD in classrooms and has yielded impressive results (Hansford et al., 2024). Their training, thinkSRSD, was a game-changer for me. I highly recommend you learn more at their website.

The topics we write about are directly related to the topics of texts we are reading during our close-reading lessons. It is powerful to have students write about what they're reading and learning about. It deepens their knowledge of and enhances their learning of the topic.

Additionally, the writing lesson provides an opportunity to integrate all foundational skills. It's not necessary to wait until students have mastered handwriting, spelling, and sentence structure. We can work on all those skills simultaneously, and they will rise together. See the pre- and post-test from one of my students below. Not only did his handwriting and spelling improve, but the quality of his writing did as well. And while there are some issues with spelling, grammar, word choice, and syntax, it is a dramatic improvement from the beginning of the year.

Name:

Date:

bats fly bats eat froot bats

Here is the pre-test from one of my first graders. It reads: "Bats fly. Bats eat fruit. Bats."

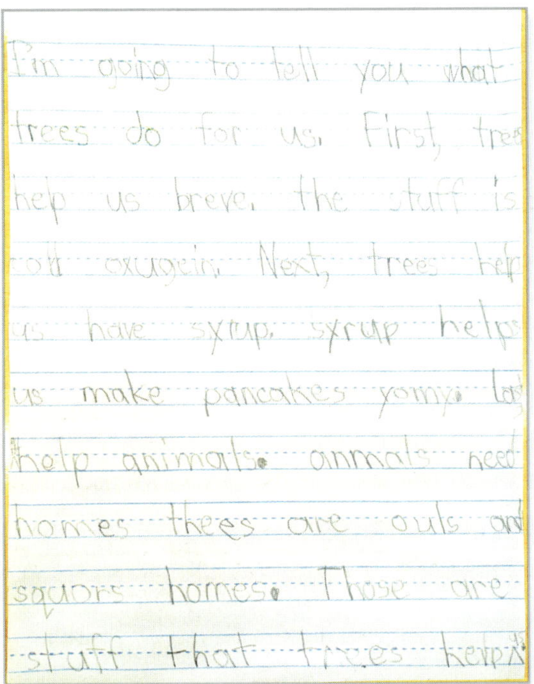
I'm going to tell you what trees do for us. First, trees help us breve. the stuff is call oxugein. Next, trees help us have syrup. syrup helps us make pancakes yomy. last help animals. animals need homes thees are ouls and squors homes. Those are stuff that trees help

Here is a post-test from the same first grader after 12 weeks of explicit writing instruction. It reads, "I'm going to tell you what trees do for us. First, trees help us breathe. The stuff is called oxygen. Next, trees help us have syrup. Syrup helps us make pancakes yummy. Last, help animals. Animals need homes. These are owls' and squirrels' homes. Those are stuff that trees help us."

Each week, I create a writing prompt that is connected to the content we are learning about in our close-reading lessons. I follow the lesson steps in this section, aiming to complete the writing process by the end of each week. Let's take a closer look at the writing portion of my literacy block, using this approach. Keep in mind that SRSD is designed to be flexible and adaptable to your specific needs. I outline my preferred lesson steps on the following pages, but adjustments and modifications are welcome so that it works for you.

BEHIND THE SCENES

Using SRSD Across Genres

The lesson steps are focused on informational writing, but I also teach narrative writing and opinion writing throughout the school year. I use SRSD across all three genres.

I remind students to go back and read what they've written to ensure it makes sense.

A Closer Look at Each Step

We cycle through the writing process each week, so each day looks a little different. I'll walk you through the steps in the first lesson, where we focus on picking our ideas and organizing them into an outline. Then I'll describe the other lessons I teach throughout the week, where we focus on writing, scoring, and setting goals. I'll show you how I put everything together at the end of the chapter in the Schedule Considerations section.

1 REVIEW POW

Day 1, whole class, on the rug or at desks, 1 minute

I start each lesson with a review of the writing process, using the mnemonic POW (Harris et al., 2003).

> **P:** pick your ideas
> **O:** organize your notes
> **W:** write

Grades 2 and up can teach the full POWeR mnemonic (Englert et al., 1991). The lowercase *e* and uppercase *R* signify the importance of revision over editing. Younger grades can introduce the eR component when students are ready.

Mnemonics, or memory aids, guide students through the writing process and help them organize their notes. The specific mnemonic isn't as crucial as the use of mnemonic devices themselves. These mnemonics alone do not create powerful writing, but they reduce the cognitive load so students can engage more deeply in the writing process (Harris, 2024). By memorizing and practicing mnemonics, students get into the habit of using them anytime they write. That is the goal, after all—for them to use the strategies to complete all steps of the writing process independently. Here's what this part of the lesson looks like:

1. I say, "What do we say to help us remember the steps of the writing process?"
2. Students say, "POW!"
3. I say, "That's right! Say it again louder and punch the air as you say it!"
4. Students say, "POW!"
5. I say, "Yes, remembering POW will help us have powerful writing! *P* stands for..."
6. Students say, "Pick your ideas!"
7. I say, "*O* stands for..."
8. Students say, "Organize your notes."
9. I say, "*W* stands for..."
10. Students say, "Write and say more!"
11. I say, "Very good. When do we use POW?"
12. Students say, "Anytime we write."

❷ REVIEW TIDE

Day 1, whole class, on the rug or at desks, 1 minute

Next, we review TIDE, which helps students organize an informational piece of writing (Mason et al., 2012). Students use TIDE when they are on the *O* step in POW.

> **T:** topic introduction
> **I:** important information
> **D:** details
> **E:** ending

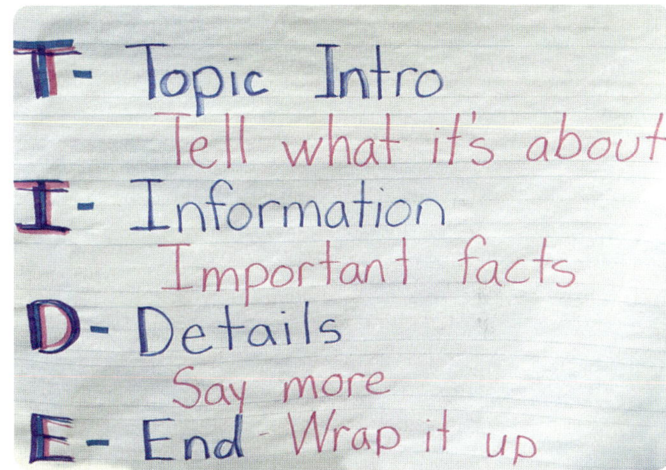

Kindergarten Version:

> **T:** topic introduction
> **ID:** important details
> **E:** ending

1. I say, "This week we'll be writing an informational piece. How do we organize our informational writing?"
2. Students say, "TIDE."
3. I say, "That's right. TIDE helps us organize the information we want to share. Let's stand up and recite our TIDE chant."
4. Students stand up and recite the following chant, with actions:
   - The topic tells what the writing's all about. (Students pat their heads.)
   - Important information; tell me more. (Students bend their right arm to flex their biceps and then extend it back out.)
   - Important information; tell me more. (Students bend their left arm to flex their biceps and then extend it back out.)
   - Important information; tell me more. (Students flex both arms at the same time.)
   - Wrap it up with an ending. (Students raise their hands out and up in a circle motion.)

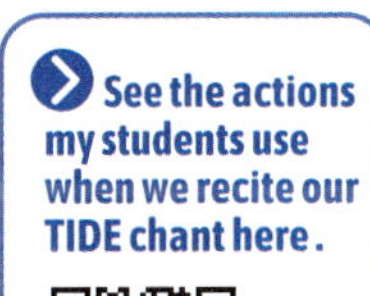

BEHIND THE SCENES

Giving Movement Breaks

To give students a movement break, I have them stand up while they say our TIDE chant.

❸ COLLABORATIVE PRACTICE: PLAN AND ORGANIZE

Day 1, whole class, on the rug or at desks, 15–20 minutes

Next, my students and I plan and organize a piece of writing. Initially, I do a lot of modeling while students follow along. But as we repeat these lessons each week (using different topics, prompts, and texts), students get more involved until they are planning, organizing, and writing independently. It's so motivating to witness this gradual release of responsibility.

In this section of the lesson, we "pull apart the prompt" (another meaning for the *P* in POW) by looking carefully at it to determine what we're being asked to do. Then we brainstorm ideas we can write about to respond to the prompt. Sometimes I list all the ideas on the whiteboard or chart paper while students

BEHIND THE SCENES

Crafting Reading-Related Writing Prompts

The reading comprehension questions in your core ELA program often work well as writing prompts. Or you can write your own. Determine a main idea/gist statement for a text you're using for close reading. Then flip that statement into a prompt. For example, after previewing some books about robots, I determined the main idea was how robots can help us in a variety of ways. Then I crafted the prompt: "Explain how robots help people."

listen, make observations, and add suggestions. Other times, I ask them to write along with me on their own sheet of paper. Finally, we circle the ideas we want to write about.

Here's what this part of the lesson might look like:

1. I pass out TIDE organizers and ask students to write POW at the top to remind them of the steps of the writing process.
2. I say, "Remember, the *P* in POW stands for 'pick your ideas.' It also stands for 'pull apart the prompt.' Let's read the writing prompt for this week."
3. We read aloud together. "Describe three organs in your body."
4. I say, "Let's pull this prompt apart. Do what?"
5. Students repeat, "Do what?" with some flair and a snap of their fingers.
6. I say, "What is this prompt asking us to do? What's the doing word?"
7. Students say, "Describe" (or whatever it might be), and we write it on the organizer.
8. Then I say, "What is it asking us to describe?"
9. Students say, "Organs in our body," or whatever the prompt is asking us to do, and we write it on the organizer.
10. I say, "Now let's pick some ideas that we can write about." Together, we discuss and list possible ideas (e.g., skin, lungs, stomach, brain, intestines). After brainstorming, we circle the ideas we like best. Students might circle the same choices I've selected, or they can choose different ideas if they are ready to write more independently.
11. I say, "Great. Now that we've pulled apart the prompt and picked our ideas, let's cross off the *P* in POW."

Next, I lead students through the next step in the writing process: *O*, or "organize your notes." We start by crafting a topic sentence together. I remind students that a topic sentence doesn't include details but tells the reader what the whole text is about. I often have students write a topic sentence by having them turn the prompt into a statement. For example, if the writing prompt is "Describe some facts about tigers," a topic sentence might be, "Here are some facts about tigers." If the writing prompt directly relates to the main idea of the text students read during the close-reading lesson, I might use the main idea/gist statement we constructed in the lesson as the topic sentence. For example, after reading a text about robots, students came up with the gist statement: "There are many different ways robots can help us." This gist sentence can become the topic sentence of a paragraph in response to the prompt, "Explain how robots help people." So I keep the main idea of the text in my mind as I craft the writing prompt.

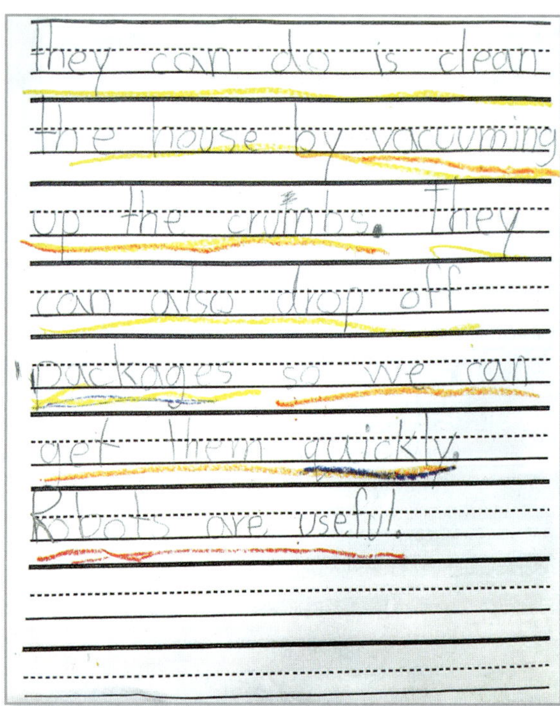

After students write the topic sentence on the organizer, we are ready to organize our ideas using TIDE. The way you use TIDE can look a little different, depending on the grade level you teach.

✱ Kindergarten Note: If you teach kindergarten, you can simplify TIDE by combining the I and D into one "important detail." Then lead students in writing 1–3 important details in the body of their writing. So the structure might look like this: T ID E or T ID ID ID E, where each ID stands for one detail. Here's an example:

> **(T)** Plants need many things to grow. **(ID)** First, you plant the seed in soil. **(ID)** Next, you give it water and sunlight. **(ID)** Last, it will grow into a beautiful plant. **(E)** We should take care of plants.

You may choose to wait to introduce TIDE until the middle of the year. Even then you can use a combination of pictures and labels to create the outline and have students participate verbally. Students can orally construct their sentences and ideas, with you serving as scribe.

✱ First-Grade Note: If you teach first grade, you have two choices for TIDE: the simple version (kindergarten, described above) or the advanced version (second grade, described below). I prefer to use the advanced version with my first graders. It's a little tough at the beginning of the year, but it gets easier in time, and it's amazing to see students rise to the challenge. You might also opt to start with the simple version, and then transition to the advanced version in the spring. Kindergarten teachers might opt to do this as well, especially if you're teaching this instruction as a verbal activity.

✱ Second-Grade Note: If you teach second grade, you can teach students to share three facts, or related nuggets of information, and then expand on each fact by sharing a related detail. The structure looks like this: T ID ID ID E, where each ID contains a fact and a thoughtful extension idea. Here's an example:

> **(T)** Egyptian pyramids are so fascinating. **(I)** They are triangular buildings built out of heavy stone blocks. **(D)** Each block weighs more than a car! **(I)** The Egyptians built pyramids to be tombs for their pharaohs. **(D)** They believed they would protect them in the afterlife. **(I)** They also filled the pyramid with treasures to take with them in the next life. **(D)** They would take weapons, jewelry, furniture, and even food. **(E)** These ancient structures are so amazing.

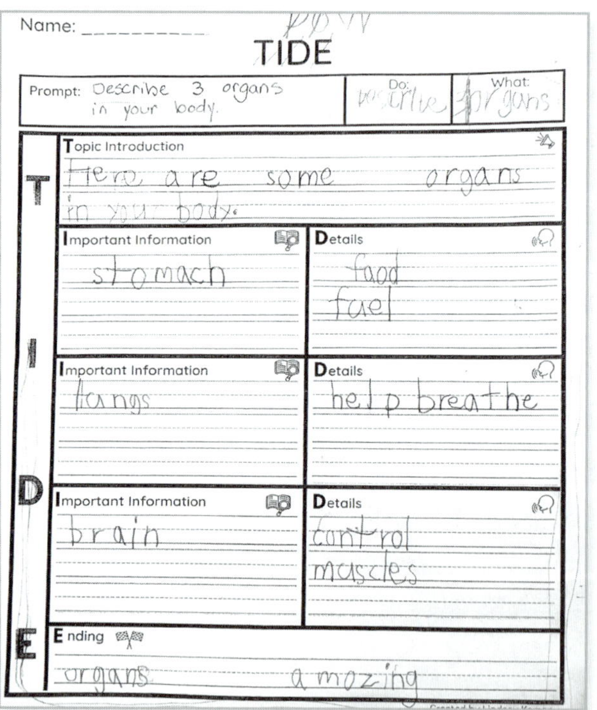

Name: __________

TIDE

Prompt: Describe 3 organs in your body. | Do: describe | What: organs

T — Topic Introduction: Here are some organs in your body.

I — Important Information: stomach | Details: food fuel

I — Important Information: lungs | Details: help breathe

D — Important Information: brain | Details: control muscles

E — Ending: organs amazing

As we fill out the TIDE organizer, we choose key words to represent our ideas and jot them down in the first column, under "Important Information" and the second column under "Details." I tell students they need to write only notes and not full sentences to conserve energy for writing a paragraph. The topic sentence is the only full sentence we write on our organizer. Then we discuss possible concluding sentences that wrap up our entire paragraph. After sharing ideas, we select a few key words to write in the "Ending" section. Once the TIDE outline is complete, we cross out the *O* in POW.

④ ORALLY REHEARSE THE PARAGRAPH

Day 1, whole class, on the rug or at desks, 5–10 minutes

Next, we use our filled-in TIDE organizer to construct a paragraph orally. I tell students that they need to be able to say it in order to *write* it. I model this for students while thinking aloud. I say my thoughts about how I might craft a paragraph, which allows students to hear my decision-making process ideas as I go. Thinking aloud is a practice emphasized in SRSD. It may feel a little awkward at first, but it gets easier the more you do it. Remember, I'm not writing yet. I'm only verbally rehearsing the paragraph. We'll write the paragraph in the next lesson. Here's what I might say:

"Now I'm ready to practice turning my TIDE outline into a paragraph. First, I will try saying what I'm going to write out loud. I'll start with the Topic Sentence. That's easy since it's written already and I can just read it. 'Here are some organs in your body.' Okay, I'm off to a great start. Now let's see what my first piece of information is. *Hmm*, it says stomach. I want to add a linking word here, so I think I'll add the word *first* since this is the first organ I'm going to talk about. Let's see. I'll say, 'The first organ I'm going to tell you about is the stomach.' I like that. Now I need to share a detail about it. My notes say, 'food fuel.' *Hmm*, I can't just write "food fuel' because it doesn't make sense. I need to turn it into a sentence: 'Food is fuel.' That kind of makes sense, but it needs

I tell students that they need to be able to say it in order to write it.

to be a detail about the stomach, so let me try again. 'The stomach turns food into fuel.' That's much better! Now I'm ready to say my second piece of information. I want to use a linking word again. 'The second organ I'm going to tell you about is the lungs.'"

I continue until I've modeled the entire paragraph. Then I give time for students to verbally craft their paragraphs with a partner as I walk around to listen and assist as needed.

I usually have time for only review, planning, organizing, and oral rehearsal on the first day of the writing cycle. Sometimes we only have time for planning and save organizing for another day. To avoid misplacing materials, I have students keep their filled-in organizers and writing paper in a bright yellow folder in their desks.

The remaining lesson steps take place on subsequent days of the week. Let's take a closer look at them.

BEHIND THE SCENES

Practicing Gradual Release

This can be challenging at the beginning of the year, so I break this down a little further. To do that, I might just model one section of the outline, and then have students practice saying just that section before moving on. For example:

1. I say, "Now let's see what my first piece of information is. *Hmm*, it says stomach. I want to add a linking word here, so I think I'll add the word *first* since this is the first organ I'm going to talk about. Let's see. I'll say, 'The first organ I'm going to tell you about is the stomach.' Now turn to your neighbor and tell them what your first sentence will be. Milks go first."
2. Students turn and talk.
3. I say, "Now I need to share a detail about it. My notes say, 'food fuel.' *Hmm*, I can't just write 'food fuel' because it doesn't make sense. I need to turn it into a sentence. 'Food is fuel.' That kind of makes sense, but it needs to be a detail about the stomach, so let me try again. 'The stomach turns food into fuel.' That's much better! Now it's your turn. Tell your neighbor what your first sentence will be. Cookies go first."
4. Students turn and talk.

5 COLLABORATIVE OR INDEPENDENT PRACTICE: WRITE

Subsequent day, whole class, at desks, 20–30 minutes

Now it's time to write! I guide students in composing sentences, using the key words from their TIDE outline. I write in front of the class while they write along with me on their own paper. As we transform each section of the TIDE organizer (e.g., "Important Information" and "Details") into a sentence, we check it off on the organizer, singing "Check it off. Check it off, off, off" to the tune of Taylor Swift's "Shake It Off"! This ensures that we include information from all parts of TIDE and helps us track our progress, easily seeing what remains to be written.

After modeling, I walk around to monitor and support students as they write independently.

Over time, students shift from writing collaboratively to writing independently. Here's a closer look at how I gradually release the responsibility to students:

- I model writing the paragraph as students watch and contribute verbally.
- Students begin to write along with me, writing on their own paper as I model. We sound out words together, and I continually give reminders about letter formation, spacing, spelling, and punctuation.
- I begin encouraging students to write different things than I do. For example, they might write a different adjective, reword a sentence, or write an entirely different piece of information or detail. I welcome and encourage their changes because it leads to independence.
- I start having students write their sentence before I write mine.
- After creating the outline together, students write the entire paragraph on their own. If there's time, I have students write during the lesson while I circle around to help, or I might pull students who need more support back to my small-group table. Another option is for students to write during their time at the writing center.

- I have students complete their TIDE organizers independently after we have pulled apart the prompt and discussed possible ideas together.
- Students do all parts of the writing process independently, including the planning, when they are ready.

Students develop independence at their own pace. It's okay if some students aren't ready for the next step toward independence. In my experience, it takes about 10 weeks of instruction before students are ready to start shifting toward some independence. Try not to rush them and, instead, provide plenty of support. I make sure to be available for those who need more scaffolding. I continue to write with students at the front of the room while other students work ahead and write on their own. When the majority of the students are ready for independence, I provide support in a small group for those who still need it.

> **✱ Kindergarten Note:** Kindergarten students can watch and verbally participate in the writing, with you as scribe. You might call on two or three students to come to the front and share the pen for a shared-writing experience. If you teach first grade, you may want to do this at the beginning of the year.

Empowering students to become self-directed writers is a magical experience.

Empowering students to become self-directed writers is a magical experience. When I first witnessed a student come up with her own topic, and then walk herself through the writing process, I knew I could never teach writing any other way. From that point on, I was hooked.

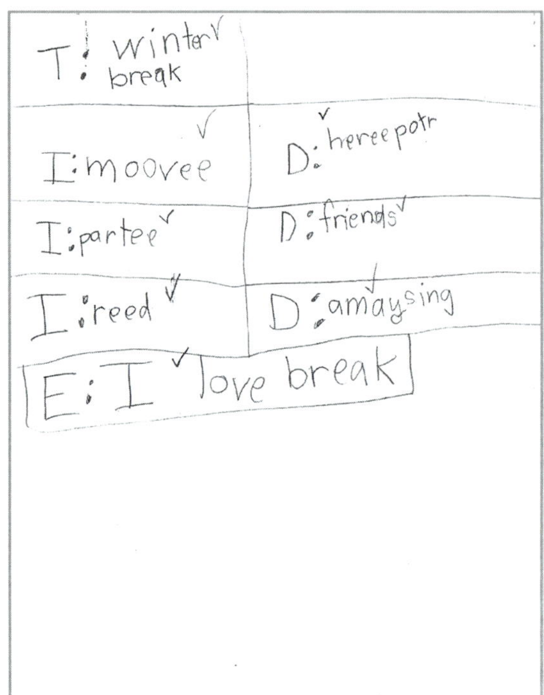

Here is a TIDE outline and corresponding paragraph that one of my first graders wrote independently at the writing center.

❻ COLOR CODE AND SCORE

Subsequent day, whole class, at desks, 15–20 minutes

In this step, we color code and score an exemplar text and our own piece from the week. For the exemplar text, I choose a text that captures the craft techniques I want students to use when they write. For example, the text might contain a nice opening hook, clear linking words, or strong vocabulary. If we are short on time one week, we might only have time to score our own writing. As students become stronger in writing and self-regulation, they score independently. Here are the steps:

Students use the TIDE rocket to score their own writing.

1. I share the exemplar text with students. We read it and discuss what we like about it, how it's structured, and any other particular features I want students to notice.
2. After the discussion, we analyze the text's parts and color code them. We underline the topic sentence in green, the important information in yellow, the details in orange, and the ending in red. We also underline strong vocabulary words and linking words in blue.
3. As we color code, I also lead students to color in parts of a TIDE rocket, which is a rubric for students to score their writing and keep track of their progress. They add stars to their rocket for each vocabulary word and a crescent-shaped moon for each linking word. We practice using the TIDE rocket by scoring the exemplar first, and then our own writing.

BEHIND THE SCENES
Using Exemplars

I tend to wait until after students have written their own text to show the exemplar text. I've found that when I show it at the beginning of the week, the students tend to copy it instead of using their own thoughts and voice. But you might find that it works well to show the exemplar text before students start writing.

4. We repeat steps 2–3, but this time color coding and scoring our own piece of writing from the week—a piece we worked on collaboratively or pieces students wrote independently. I remind them that the purpose of scoring is to determine growth. It's okay if they missed something because that just means they know what to work on the next time they write.

✱ Kindergarten Note: If you teach kindergarten, use just three colors when color coding: green for "topic sentence," yellow for "details," and red for "ending."

7 SET GOALS

Subsequent day, whole class, at desks, 5 minutes

An important part of SRSD is setting goals regularly. In this step, we review our writing from the week, as well as the TIDE rocket, to determine goals we need to set. We prioritize including all TIDE components in initial goals. For students who omit any part, their goal becomes incorporating all the parts of TIDE. Once students are able to consistently include all these parts, I encourage them to set other goals, such as using strong vocabulary words, linking words, or a strong opening hook. Students might also set an editing goal, such as remembering capitals, punctuation, or word spacing. I have my students write their goals on sticky notes and display them on a class poster, replacing goals as they meet them each week.

✱ Second-Grade Note: I suggest adding peer scoring after students have self-scored. I start doing this at the end of first grade if I feel students are ready—and it's impressive to hear them respectfully give advice to one another. Here are the steps:

1. Students greet their partner with a smile.
2. Partner 1 reads his writing to Partner 2 and shares a goal. For example, he might say, "My goal is to have a strong hook at the beginning." Or "My goal is to get all the parts of TIDE."
3. Partner 1 rereads the piece, stopping after each section. Partner 2:
   - Gives a compliment.
   - Gives a score and explains why (colors in the rocket part or not).
   - Gives suggestions.
4. Partners switch roles and repeat Steps 1–3.
5. Both students reflect and set goals.

The purpose of scoring our writing is to identify areas for growth, which helps students set specific writing goals.

Those are the core writing lessons for each week. If I have time, I add a lesson on revision. I typically display a below-standard example of writing, which I create or use from a previous student (with the name removed). Then the students and I choose one part to revise. When I write a below-standard example, I often purposefully leave out an important part, such as the topic sentence. Then we revise the paper by collectively writing a topic sentence. Here are the steps:

1. I locate or write the below-standard exemplar and give each student a copy.
2. We read it and discuss what we like.
3. We color code and score it, using the TIDE rocket, to determine if it has all important parts.
4. We choose an especially problematic part and revise it together.

BEHIND THE SCENES

Crafting Reading-Related Writing Prompts 2

Each week, create a prompt that you can use to instruct and lead students through the writing process. To do that, review the comprehension questions in your ELA core program and consider how they might be used for the writing prompt. Many programs include an essential question or theme to focus on each week that can be turned into a writing prompt. Another option is to review the texts you are reading in your close-reading lessons. Determine which one you'll be reading at the beginning of the week and craft a prompt related to it. You can craft a prompt by creating a gist statement and flipping it into a question.

BEHIND THE SCENES

Collect Student Samples

I collect student below-standard, standard, and above-standard writing samples throughout the year to use as exemplars. Before the lesson, I remove the name to protect student privacy. Here's a wonderful piece that one of my first graders wrote independently. She just left out an additional detail for her third piece of information about how robots can drop off packages. I would copy this piece in black and white, and have students color code it to determine the missing detail. Then we brainstorm a way she might have extended her thinking. For example, she might have explained why it's useful for robots to drop off packages.

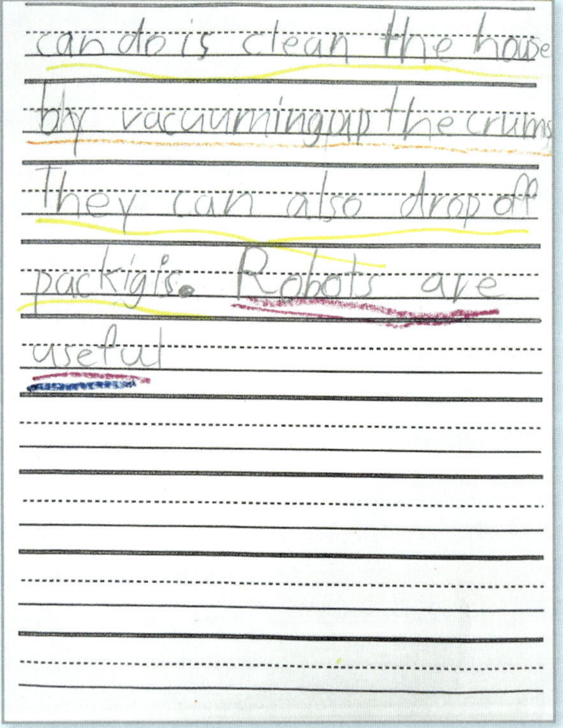

Schedule Considerations: Finding Your Groove

My ideal schedule includes 30 minutes of dedicated writing instruction each day, which enables students to work through the POW writing process each week, and wind up with a finished piece. But occasionally time limitations prevent me from going beyond planning and organizing. Here's what my ideal schedule might look like.

Monday	Tuesday	Wednesday	Thursday	Friday
30 minutes	30 minutes	30 minutes	30 minutes	20 minutes
Collaborative Practice: Plan and Organize	**Collaborative or Independent Practice: Write**	**Collaborative or Independent Practice: Write**	**Color Code, Score, Set Goals**	**Revise**

And here's an example of when time limitations prevented that: One year, I had PE and music scheduled on Mondays, which cut into our writing time. So I integrated writing into my close-reading lesson. Here's what that looked like.

Monday	Tuesday	Wednesday	Thursday	Friday
	30 minutes	20 minutes	30 minutes	20 minutes
Writing Combined With Close Reading: Read a text together and write a gist statement (see Chapter 4, page 73 for details).	**Collaborative Practice: Plan and Organize**	**Collaborative Practice: Write**	**Collaborative Practice: Write**	**Color Code, Score, Set Goals**

Writing is one of the most demanding tasks students engage in. Not only do they need to engage in deep-processing to choose a topic, come up with important information and details, organize them, construct meaningful sentences to compose one or more paragraphs, and self-regulate, they also need to attend to the foundational skills of handwriting, spelling, and grammar. It's a monumental task!

To ensure students develop all of those skills, I teach writing, as well as writing-related processes, not only during a dedicated time each day but also throughout the literacy block. Let's take a look.

Arrival: I build oral language through conversations. See Chapter 2.

Phonics: I embed handwriting and spelling instruction here. We also work on conventions such as capitalization, punctuation, and spacing during sentence dictation. See Chapter 3.

Close Reading: I build oral language, vocabulary, and knowledge, which all impact writing heavily. I embed sentence-level instruction (such as sentence expansion, sentence combining, sentence variety, etc.) when students are writing gist statements. I integrate handwriting and spelling as they write statements, too, as well as summaries and responses to texts. Students choose vocabulary words they are learning to use in their TIDE outlines. See Chapter 4.

Writing: In addition to bringing all writing components together, we learn strategies to help us with the writing process, self-regulation, and the selected genre.

Small Groups and Centers: Students practice applying all the skills they are learning during the writing center. I address specific needs, such as letter formation, during my small-group instruction. See Chapter 6.

In Closing, Remember...

SRSD is an evidence-based approach to writing instruction that includes not only teaching writing strategies but also self-regulation strategies. Each week, a writing prompt is given that is connected to the content students are learning in close-reading lessons. Students are led through a cycle of steps that include planning, organizing, writing, scoring, and setting goals. They receive instruction that utilizes explicit teaching, modeling, and think-alouds, while also encouraging them to collaborate and participate in discussions. Scaffolds are faded as students begin to move toward independence.

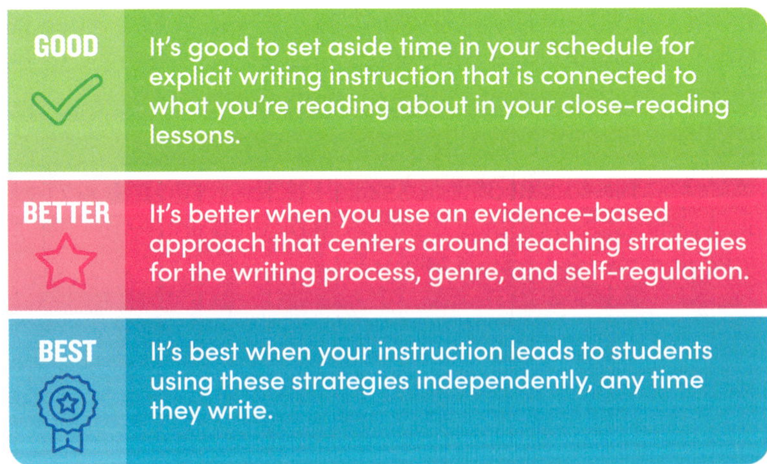

Turning Up the Volume: Small Groups and Centers

CHAPTER 6

SPOTLIGHT ON SMALL GROUPS AND CENTERS

When students come in from recess, they go to either the reading, writing, or technology center first. While they're busy working independently in centers, I invite small groups of students to my reading table. We may start with word-level skills, but the true magic is when students apply those skills to reading books! I love listening to my students read and providing immediate, individualized feedback. It is not only valuable to them, but it is also valuable to me because I get to know them deeply as readers.

DOMINANT MOVES FROM *7 MIGHTY MOVES*

MOVE 1: Teach Phonemic Awareness With Intention

MOVE 2: Teach Phonics Explicitly and Systematically

MOVE 3: Teach Decoding Strategies, Not Cueing Strategies

MOVE 4: Use Decodable Texts Instead of Predictable Texts With Beginning Readers

MOVE 5: Embrace a Better Approach to Teaching "Sight Words"

MOVE 6: Focus on Meaningful Fluency Practice

MOVE 7: Improve Comprehension by Developing Vocabulary and Background Knowledge

A Closer Look at Small-Group Instruction

I use small groups and centers as a time to reinforce concepts I've taught in my whole-class phonics lessons. I also use them to tailor practice opportunities for students based on their needs and to provide immediate, individualized feedback. I prioritize things that I can't do as easily in whole-class instruction. If I *do* repeat something I did with the whole class, it's because students need a double dose of that instruction or practice to reach mastery. If I were to only teach students to read as a whole class, I might not pick up on a child's specific needs, such as blending sounds into a word or struggling to recall a certain letter sound. But when I work with that child in a small group, I can hear his struggle and assist him. This is why I find small-group instruction especially useful in the earliest grades.

Lindsay Live! Enter her classroom to learn more about small groups and centers.

Small-Group Focal Points

- Alphabet Knowledge
- Decoding
- Fluency
- Vocabulary and Comprehension

Centers

- Reading Center
- Technology Center
- Writing Center

Assessment drives my grouping decisions. Different groups have different purposes. I tailor each group based on student needs, as determined by formal and informal assessment data. At the beginning of the year, I use our reading benchmark screener to determine the areas with which students need the most help. I then create groups of four or five students each, accordingly. From there, I adjust the placements as I work with students to better understand their needs. These groups are fluid and ever-changing.

While we work on several skills in each group, I always have a primary focus:

- alphabet knowledge
- decoding
- fluency
- vocabulary/comprehension

Listen and notice the scaffolding I do to help a brand-new reader blend sounds into words. This kind of focused, individualized support is possible when working with small groups.

Let's look at each one.

FOCUS ON ALPHABET KNOWLEDGE

I group students who are still learning the names, sounds, and formations of alphabet letters. When I taught kindergarten, the majority of students required focused attention in this area, so I organized students into subgroups based on the approximate number of letters they knew (e.g., five or fewer, around 10, around 20). A common recommendation is to group students who are missing the same letters, but that is impractical, I've found, given the vast array of letter combinations. Typically, students with little alphabet knowledge require extended practice. So by grouping based on the overall number of mastered letters, I can devote more practice time to students who need it. Of course, when some students start to master letters more quickly than others in their group, I move them to a more advanced group.

Another important consideration is the students' level of phonemic awareness—the understanding that spoken language can be broken down into individual speech sounds (phonemes). I've found that many students who struggle to learn the alphabet, also struggle with phonemic awareness.

Working with students in small groups allows me to tailor my instruction and feedback to students' needs.

So I dedicate time in small groups to work on blending and segmenting phonemes. If there are several students who do not have this need, I divide the group into a strictly alphabet knowledge group and an alphabet knowledge with phonemic awareness group.

BEHIND THE SCENES

Setting Up for Phonemic Awareness Practice

Prior to calling students back, I have the manipulatives we'll use for our phonemic awareness practice at each place. Manipulatives are a scaffold, so if students don't need them anymore, I don't set them out.

Here's a possible lesson outline for this focus area.

1. Phonemic Awareness Practice (e.g., blending, segmenting, word chains)
2. Alphabet Chant
3. Review: Visual Drill and Auditory Drill
4. Letter Formation Instruction and Practice
5. Word Reading Practice
6. Beginner Decodable Books Practice

Let's take a deeper dive into the routines I utilize during this group and the transitions between lesson parts. The times below reflect a 15-minute group. If I have more or less time to work with students during this time, I adjust the minutes spent per step. The amount of time I spend with each group varies, depending on the needs of the group and the time available. I spend more time with the students who need me the most. (See "Schedule Considerations" on page 141 for more.)

I carry out all small-group activities at the reading table, which students can rotate to and from easily.

First, I call students' names to come to my small-group table. I prefer a kidney-shaped table because it allows me to easily reach all students and fosters a sense of focus as everyone faces me.

1. Phonemic Awareness Practice

1–2 minutes

I might choose to practice blending or segmenting during a lesson, or I might include both. Using manipulatives during phonemic awareness practice can be a great scaffold for students, and they are also a fun way to add variety to the routines. But to effectively use them, ensure they directly support your learning objectives and are introduced with clear instructions and modeling. Establish clear rules and routines for managing them to minimize distractions and ensure efficient use of time. Intervene promptly

BEHIND THE SCENES

Helping Struggling Students

If phonemic awareness is a struggle for students, increase the amount of time on it before moving on. Also consider scaffolds, such as using words with continuous sounds, fewer phonemes, and picture support.

Using manipulatives is one way to scaffold students as they learn how to segment the phonemes in words. Scaffolds are temporary and should be removed when students no longer need them.

if students use the manipulatives in ways they are not intended to be used or are distracting other students. They should increase the learning, not reduce it. If the efficiency of your lesson is decreased by the use of the manipulatives, you may need to reevaluate their use.

1. I say, "I'll say a word and then you'll say it and "pop" the sounds in the word. Ready? *mat*."
2. Students say, "/m/ /a/ /t/" while they push a pop-it for each sound.
3. I say, "Flip it" to direct students to flip over the pop-its in preparation for the next word.
4. I repeat with 5-9 more words.

2. Alphabet Chant

1 minute

Next, I lead students in chanting the alphabet. Each student has an alphabet page in front of them. They point to the capital letter as they say the name, the lowercase letter as they say the name, then they say the sound of the letter while doing an action I have taught them. It sounds like this: "*A, a, /a/; B, b, /b/; C, c, /k/,*" and so on.

TRANSITION TIP

Manage Materials

Before I call students over, I have the alphabet pages in a pile right in front of me. As soon as we are done segmenting, I sweep up the pop-its with my arm so students are not distracted by them and quickly place the alphabet boards in front of students. While students are chanting the alphabet, I put the pop-its away in a basket behind me. Then I pick up the grapheme deck so I'm ready for the visual drill that comes next.

3. Review: Visual and Auditory Drills

3–5 minutes

Learning the alphabet involves associating a name and a sound with a written symbol. These associations are made from visual to verbal and verbal to visual (Roberts et al., 2019). The visual and auditory drills are a critical part of this small-group lesson for these students because it gives them so many opportunities to go back and forth between the visual form of the letter and the verbal representations (name, sound). Let's look closer.

Visual Drill

The visual drill is an opportunity for students to see a grapheme and state the associated sound(s). I include letters students already know, plus some letters they are still learning. Initially, I'll use cards that have both the capital and lowercase letters on each card. As students progress, I'll change to cards with the capital and lowercase letters on separate cards. I'll flip through the cards and have students say the letter sounds. Then I flip through again to have them say the letter names. When all students in the group have mastered a letter, I'll remove it from the deck to make room for new cards. This drill might take 1–2 minutes.

TRANSITION TIP

Prep for Drills

Before I call students over, I have my deck of grapheme cards in front of me as well as the words written on the whiteboard. I quickly gather up the alphabet pages and have the cards ready to go.

BEHIND THE SCENES

Targeting Practice

You can target a letter in this drill that students are learning. For example, if the students are still learning the name and sound for *b*, you can continually add this sound into the drill. Your order might look like the following: /m/ /b/ /a/ /l/ /b/ /g /t/ /i/ /b/. Students get multiple repetitions to help them make the letter-sound connection.

Auditory Drill

The auditory drill is when I say a sound and students write the letter(s) that represents that sound. I love to have students use sand trays during small group to practice letter names, sounds, and correct formation. I find value in having students use this multisensory method, which involves the visual, auditory, and tactile-kinesthetic sensory systems, when learning the alphabet. While we don't have research yet that compares instruction with and without a multisensory component (Birsh, 2018), I find that it helps students focus carefully on how they form their letters. This is also something that researchers Berninger and Wolf claim (2015). I also like that students build a link between the grapheme they see, the phoneme they hear, what they feel in their mouths as they produce the sound, and what they feel in their hands and fingers as they write. Plus, it's fun! Students always look forward to working with the sand. But you don't have to use the multisensory method. An individual whiteboard with a marker or a piece of paper and pencil work fine. In this drill, I say a sound, and students repeat the sound and then form the lowercase letter.

Here's the routine.

1. I say, "The sound is /b/."
2. Students say, "/b/; *b* spells /b/" while they write the letter in the sand.
3. I say, "Shake it out."
4. Students carefully shake the sand trays to erase their letter and prepare for the next one.
5. I say, "The sound is /m/."
6. Students say, "/m/; *m* spells /m/" while they write the letter in the sand.
7. I say, "Shake it out." Students shake out their trays.
8. I say, "The sound is /a/."
9. Students say, "/a/; *a* spells /a/" while they write the letter in the sand.
10. I repeat with about 5-8 more sounds.

I watch students as they form their letters. I immediately correct students if I see them start the letter in the wrong spot (e.g., at the bottom instead of at the top), write a letter backwards, etc. Then I'll have them practice writing that letter again to help them remember the correct handwriting pathway.

TRANSITION TIP

Manage Sand Trays

After the visual drill, I pass out a tray
of sand to each child. I have important
guidelines f[...] students to ensure that
usi[...] is an efficient use of
[...]ts are not allowed to
[...]nd tray. It needs to
[...] table so nothing
[...]how to gently "shake
[...] sure the tray is flat.
[...]owed to put one
[...]sand. They cannot
[...]owed to write the
[...]n. If students

struggle to follow the rules, I kindly, but firmly, take their trays away. Then they complete the auditory drill by tracing their finger on the table or writing on a whiteboard. I always let students know that they can try again next time—and they almost always do better. These rules are important so that working with sand does not distract students from the targeted learning that needs to take place. If you find the sand trays are too much to manage, it's best to use individual whiteboards or paper.

4. Letter Formation Instruction and Practice

2 minutes

To solidify letter formation, I guide students in writing letters with a pencil or with a dry-erase marker. I model and remind students how to form the letter and then have them write it. If I want students to have more time to practice their decodable book, I omit this step since students practiced letter formation in the auditory drill.

TRANSITION TIP

Lean on PowerPoint

As in earlier parts of the day, my preparation can make the transitions during small-group instruction seamless. When I'm finished working with students, I have them quietly look up at the PowerPoint presentation to identify the center they need to return to. (See more on page 131.)

5. Word Reading Practice

1–3 minutes

I model how to blend a word, and then I have students blend words that I have written on my small whiteboard; or I give students a word list, and we practice reading the words together.

BEHIND THE SCENES

Selecting Books

I select decodable books before school so I don't have to waste small-group time finding the right books.

6. Beginner Decodable Books Practice

5–8 minutes

I have students practice reading aloud from a simple decodable text, ensuring the text only includes the letters students have been taught.

FOCUS ON DECODING

Students in this group are in full-on decoding-mode! They know basic letter-sound relationships, and are working to solidify new phonics concepts, such as digraphs and vowel teams, as I teach them. I give students plenty of opportunities to apply those concepts in connected text to develop automaticity with phonics skills. The majority of my first graders benefit from this work. I might further divide groups by looking at who needs phonemic-awareness support and who does not, as well as how many correct letter sounds in a minute they get on a reading screener. Then I group students with similar needs/scores.

During the majority of our small-group time, we focus on reading books. This allows students ample practice reading connected text with my feedback and support.

Here's a possible lesson outline for this focus area:

1. Phonemic Awareness Practice (e.g., blending, segmenting, word chains)
2. Review Target Letter Pattern
3. Read/Write Words That Contain the Target Letter Pattern
4. Pre-Teach or Review Irregular High-Frequency Words or Vocabulary Words
5. Read Decodable Text (Most of the time is spent here.)
6. Ask Questions About or Retell the Text

Let's look closer at what typically happens in this group if I have 12 minutes to work with them.

1. Phonemic Awareness Practice

1 minute

As I did for the alphabet knowledge group, I have students practice blending and/or segmenting during the lesson. Or I might start things off with a word chain.

1. I say, "Are you ready to be word detectives? I'm going to say the sounds in a word, and you'll figure out what the word is. /s/ /u/ /n/."
2. Students say, "sun."
3. I repeat with 5–9 more words

2. Review Target Letter Pattern

< 1 minute

Decodable texts usually focus on a specific target skill. I show students the target skill (e.g., *ch*) and ask them what sound it represents. I tell them that our book today will have a lot of words with this target spelling.

BEHIND THE SCENES

Choosing Words Strategically

The types of words I use depend on the needs of my students. If they are struggling to blend words with three sounds, I use three-sound words with continuous sounds before moving on to words with stop sounds. If three sounds are easy for them, I use words with four sounds. Use words from the decodable text students are going to read or words from the phonemic awareness word lists in *7 Mighty Moves Reading Resources*.

3. Read/Write Words That Contain the Target Letter Pattern

1–2 minutes

Next, we read or write words that contain the target skill. I pass out word lists to students and have them start reading aloud. I listen and provide support when needed.

BEHIND THE SCENES

Previewing the Decodable Text

Before I call students over, I preview the decodable text for any irregular high-frequency words or tricky vocabulary words and write them on my small dry-erase board.

4. Pre-Teach or Review Irregular High-Frequency Words or Vocabulary Words

2 minutes

I quickly pre-teach or review any words that might challenge students as they read the decodable text. I will also help them with any vocabulary words that are critical to comprehending the text.

Here's what I might say for the high-frequency words *saw* and *they*.

"You will see this word in our story today. (Point to the word.) The *a-w* spells the sound /aw/. What sound? (/aw/). That's right. Let's sound out the word together. /s/ /aw/. *Saw*. Yes, we haven't learned that yet, so that's a little tricky.

Here's another word you will see in our story. This is the word *they*. What word? (*they*). Yes, which two letters spell the /th/ sound? That's right, *t-h*. Which two letters are spelling the /ay/ sound in this word? Yes, the letters *e-y* spell /ay/ in this word. That is tricky. Let's sound it out again. /th/ /ay/, *they*.

Now when I point to one of our words, you say it. Ready?" (I switch off pointing to the words and having students read them in unison.)

5. Read Decodable Text

9 minutes

This is where I like to spend the majority of the time in the lesson. If students don't need support with phonemic awareness or the extra practice with word lists, then I skip those steps and get right to reading. Also, if I'm short on time one day, I skip those steps and get right to reading. I stagger-start students

I love listening to and supporting my students as they read.

so that they are all reading aloud but at different places in the text. That way students are not just echoing what their neighbors say. If students finish the book, they start it again so that the task is never-ending. They keep reading until I say to stop. As they read, I lean in to listen and provide feedback. This is my favorite part of the day! Helping students, particularly those learning to read, is so fulfilling. My support is essential for them as they navigate the challenging task of recalling sounds and blending them together.

TRANSITION TIP

Stagger Student Reading

I give a book to every other student at the table. For example, if there are five students, I give a book to the students in spots 1, 3, and 5, and ask those three students to start reading aloud. I have students 2 and 4 read the target-skill word list. Once students 1, 3, and 5 finish the first page or paragraph, I hand books to students 2 and 4 to begin reading.

6. Ask Questions About or Retell the Text

1–2 minutes

I ask students questions about the text or have them retell the story with a partner.

FOCUS ON FLUENCY

Students who are ready for small-group instruction in fluency tend to read with more automaticity and accuracy than those in the decoding group. While they still may be working to solidify some phonics skills, they are ready to receive focused support in phrasing, rate, and expression. While I might use decodable texts with students initially, I work on transitioning them into less decodable books, and then into regular, authentic books.

To determine if students are ready for small-group instruction in fluency, I look at their wcpm (words correct per minute) score and accuracy score on a reading passage from my reading benchmark screener. I also make a note of the way they read—whether they read with expression and prosody, or not. If students have a low accuracy score, I will put them in the decoding group. If their accuracy is adequate, but their wcpm score is low, they are a great candidate for a fluency group. If their wcpm is average or above average, but

they read in a monotone or robotic way, they are also a good candidate for the fluency group.

Here's a possible lesson outline for this focus area.

1. Review Target Letter Pattern (if needed)
2. Read/Write Words That Contain the Target Letter Pattern (if needed)
3. Pre-Teach or Review Irregular High-Frequency or Vocabulary Words
4. Read Text (Most of the time is spent here.)
5. Ask Questions About or Retell the Text

BEHIND THE SCENES
Adjusting Instruction

You do not need to follow these lesson steps rigidly. If your students do not need extra instruction in phonemic awareness or the target skill, skip these steps and get right to introducing the text and reading. Follow the needs and data of your students.

Because this outline is similar to the outline for decoding (pages 117–119), I don't go into great detail about instruction here or in the sections that follow. The main differences are in the type of text I use (decodable, less decodable, or authentic) and in the instruction I give students while listening to them read.

For example, I might engage students in an activity I call, "Read, Model, Read Again." After a student reads aloud a paragraph or page, I model the same portion of the text for the student, while they track with their finger. I demonstrate appropriate rate, phrasing, and expression. After I model, the student rereads the same portion of text. This allows them another opportunity to read, which gives them more exposure to the words, develops fluency, and builds confidence. Another strategy I might use is to read the text in unison with the student, reading slightly quicker than they typically read. This is useful for students who are accurate readers, but need a little boost in their reading rate and prosody. (See Move 6 in *7 Mighty Moves*, page 118.)

I listen carefully to students as they read to help me determine if the text is appropriate for them. If students resort to a lot of guessing, I know I need to put them into an easier, more decodable text. If the students breeze through the text easily, I know that I can consider a more difficult text to challenge them. Depending on the needs of the students, I may be able to skip reading/writing words that contain the target skill.

FOCUS ON VOCABULARY AND COMPREHENSION

For students who are strong, fluent readers, I focus on building vocabulary, background knowledge, and comprehension through rich texts. That doesn't mean I don't address vocabulary and comprehension in the alphabet knowledge, decoding, and fluency groups. But, for this group, they're the primary focus. In this group I also allow time for students to respond to the text in writing to deepen their thinking and improve their writing skills.

Give students appropriately challenging texts when they're ready for them.

Students in this group meet or exceed grade-level benchmarks in both wcpm and accuracy. If they do not have strong retell scores, I can subdivide the group to focus on students who need support in retelling.

Here's a possible lesson outline for this group.

1. Pre-Teach Vocabulary Words
2. Activate/Build Background Knowledge
3. Read the Text
4. Question, Retell, and Discuss the Text
5. Respond to the Text in Writing

Let's take a closer look at what this would look like if I had 15 minutes to work with this group.

1. Pre-Teach Vocabulary Words

1–2 minutes

I briefly introduce any unknown vocabulary words or words that students may struggle to read.

2. Activate/Build Background Knowledge

1–2 minutes

We discuss any concepts that are necessary for students to know to comprehend the text. I also introduce the text to students.

3. Read the Text

8–10 minutes

I might choose to read the text simultaneously with students so that we are all at the same point in it. Because these students are fluent and focusing on comprehension, I model how to think aloud as we read. I also help to build students' understanding of the text *as we read*, instead of simply asking questions when we're finished. I can stop at points to model and have students practice a particular strategy, such as asking questions or summarizing.

Or I might assign students to read the text independently when they are at the reading center. Then we meet in a small group. That way, we have more time to spend on discussion and writing in response to the text.

4. Question, Retell, and Discuss the Text

3–5 minutes

I ask students questions and we discuss the text. Some of this is done while we are reading. We craft a gist statement together (see page 73),

5. Respond to the Text in Writing

2+ minutes

Students write a gist statement, which means they summarize the text into one main-idea sentence. I may also give them a writing prompt that relates to the text.

OTHER NEEDS

Sometimes I group students based on other areas of need. This might include English learners who need foundational Tier 1 vocabulary in addition to alphabet knowledge/decoding, or students with cognitive delays who benefit from extra attention on basic skills. I also identify students who struggle with short vowels or with letter reversals like *b* and *d*, providing them with targeted instruction and practice. By using formal and informal assessments, I can determine if there are certain skill gaps that warrant grouping beyond alphabet knowledge, decoding, fluency, and comprehension/vocabulary.

A Closer Look at Centers—or What the Other Students Are Doing

Small groups ensure differentiation, personalized attention and focused learning for students, which is supported by research (Puzio et al., 2020). But what about the other students? We want them to be engaged in meaningful activities as well, but this can be challenging when they're not working directly with the teacher. To address that, I plan beneficial center activities where students can work independently or with a parent volunteer or a paraprofessional (if I'm able to recruit them).

Centers provide students with a bit of a break from the more intense instruction that happens in the other parts of our day. It's important to remember that learning to read and write is hard work and cognitively exhausting for many students. So giving them 15 minutes to, for example, listen to an audiobook provides them with a little downtime while providing a positive experience with books and an opportunity to hear rich literature, often with advanced vocabulary.

Also, I believe the benefits of working with students in small groups outweigh the potential costs, especially in grades K–2 since these students need a lot of support and practice in foundational skills, with a teacher, to learn how to read. We just need to be mindful of the amount of time students are without a teacher and the activities they're engaged in.

Having said all that, when possible, I recruit volunteers to run reading groups, which maximizes the amount of time students are working with an adult and minimizes the independent work time.

I prefer center activities that require minimum prep. I'm all about easy-to-plan activities because so much of my time is focused on planning instruction that I lead throughout the day. So let's dive into the three main centers you'll see in my classroom, during small-group instruction: reading center, technology center, and writing center.

READING CENTER

I provide a classroom library of books to peruse and read. Students love looking through the wide selection of books and rereading (or just looking at) books that I've read aloud to the class. Some students can read independently, but of course many more are still learning to decode. Regardless of their reading abilities, all students have the option to listen to audiobooks during this time. I use the Epic app, a database of digital books. The app in many of those books highlight the text while reading it aloud to students. This is a great opportunity for students to enjoy stories and build knowledge while being exposed to rich literature, interesting themes, and more advanced language and vocabulary.

BEHIND THE SCENES

Putting Books Over Videos

In the Epic app, I disable the "video" feature under settings. That way, students can only access books, and not videos, during the reading center.

Students enjoy having the choice to read or listen to books during the reading center.

I used to frown upon any talking during this time. But I've come to recognize the importance of building positive reading experiences for students and the value of positive interactions among students. I love when I see two of them giggling as they experience a book together on the bean bag. Sometimes one student reads aloud a book to another student who isn't able to read it themself. Other times I see students take turns as they tackle the book together. The special bonding moments I witness at this center are priceless.

My books are organized by genre, theme, or author. For example, some of the categories include: animals, dinosaurs, Froggy books, fairy tales, Eric Carle, Pete the Cat books, and more.

BEHIND THE SCENES
Using "Bookmarks"

I use paint sticks to create large numbered "bookmarks" for students. Students place their bookmarks in the bins from which they have removed books. That way, they know exactly which bins to return their books to when center time ends.

TECHNOLOGY CENTER

In the technology center, students use a reading software program called Lexia, which enables students to work on specific skills they need. They can go at their own pace, and the software differentiates instruction for me!

Students receive differentiated instruction at the Technology Center.

BEHIND THE SCENES

Celebrating Milestones

Lexia allows me to monitor my students' progress. When students complete a milestone, I print out the certificates they've earned and pass them out as part of our morning routine. I encourage students to clap and cheer for each other when I announce their names. It helps to keep students motivated as they work in the program. I'm also able to log in and see any concepts students may be struggling with. I make a note of these things so that I can address them in my small-group instruction.

WRITING CENTER

Students have a few options in the writing center. First, they work on a piece that we've started in our whole-class writing lesson. Then, I have a variety of types of paper for them to choose from. Once they've chosen a type of paper, they make a card, write a letter, complete a handwriting page, write a story, or construct sentences to match a pre-printed picture. To ensure students produce high-quality work, I limit the number of sheets students can take each day to two, which encourages them to focus on quality over quantity.

BEHIND THE SCENES
Capturing Writing

Keep students accountable by having them photograph their writing and record themselves reading it, using an app such as Seesaw. By having caregivers at home connect to the app, you give students an authentic audience to write for and keep them motivated. Plus, caregivers love seeing what their child is working on at school.

✱ Kindergarten Note: In kindergarten, the writing center might include paper for drawing, coloring, cutting, and tracing. It might also include other fine motor activities to help strengthen students' hand muscles, precision, and coordination in preparation for writing.

OTHER CENTERS

Here are centers I don't include as regularly but can be beneficial to students.

Word Work Center

At this center, I provide a variety of phonics games for students to play to review and reinforce previously taught skills. Full disclosure: During COVID, I had to eliminate this center because I couldn't have students sharing materials, and I now find that I don't really miss it. It was nice not to have to prep the materials, and my students didn't seem to need it because their learning was still on target. Looking back, I realize this was the center where they would most likely get off task. Now, I only include this center when I have a parent volunteer who can run it and ensure students are making good use of their time.

Students play a game from *7 Mighty Moves Reading Resources* at the Word Work Center.

BEHIND THE SCENES

Modeling Voice Levels

I model appropriate voice levels for students at the Explore Center. While I encourage friendly conversation, it's important to keep the noise level manageable. This allows students working with me in small groups to concentrate on their reading without distractions.

Explore Center

The Explore Center is a hands-on station I used in kindergarten. In first and second grades, I only include this center on Fridays. Here, students can explore a variety of STEM materials, a light table, puppets, or even a play kitchen. It's a fun and engaging way for them to work on language development, social skills, creativity, problem-solving, and critical thinking.

Students look forward to the Explore Center on Fridays.

Managing Small Groups and Centers

Now that I've explained what students are doing with me in small groups, as well as what the other students are doing, let's put everything together. I plan and schedule centers a few ways, inspired by Tara West (2017), depending on the needs of my students, the number of adults available to assist me, and the amount of time I have on that particular day. I'll start by describing Variation 1, which is the variation of centers I begin with at the beginning of the year. A description of the other two variations follow.

CENTERS VARIATION 1

My centers run smoothly thanks to PowerPoint slides. Yes, slides! Each one represents a round of centers. I typically have the three core centers displayed, with students' names beneath them. Each center is 15 minutes long. In kindergarten, each center is about 10 minutes long.

Project a Go-To Center Guide

I open up and project the PowerPoint presentation while students are at recess. As they come in, they can quickly look up on the screen to identify their first center. The different colors help them find their names quickly.

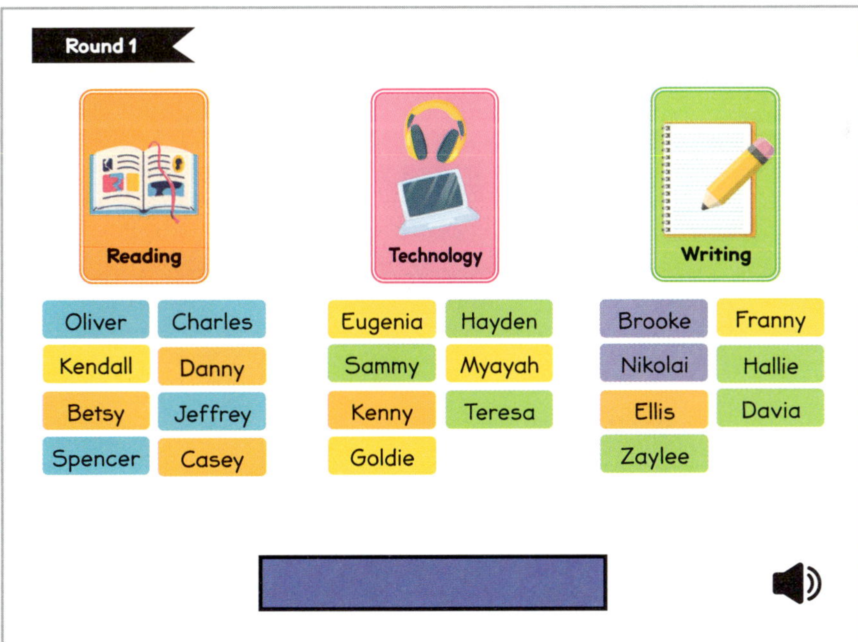

BEHIND THE SCENES

Tapping the Power of PowerPoint

Everything runs on its own. Once students are trained, I simply start the PowerPoint and can focus on small groups. I don't need to tell students outside the group with which I'm working when to switch centers because the PowerPoint does it for me. This makes substitute plans super easy. I just leave directions for the sub on how to display and start the PowerPoint, and she's good to go!

The blue bar at the bottom is a visual timer. Once I start the PowerPoint presentation, the bar is white and gradually fills in blue as the minutes go by. Students can look at this bar to see how much time is left in their center. When the bar is almost completely filled in, they know it is almost time to change centers. At 15 minutes, music plays to let students know that it is time to switch. They clean up and quickly get to their next center, aiming to be there before the music stops. Then the visual timer starts all over again as students start work at their second center. After 15 minutes, the process repeats, and students move to their third center.

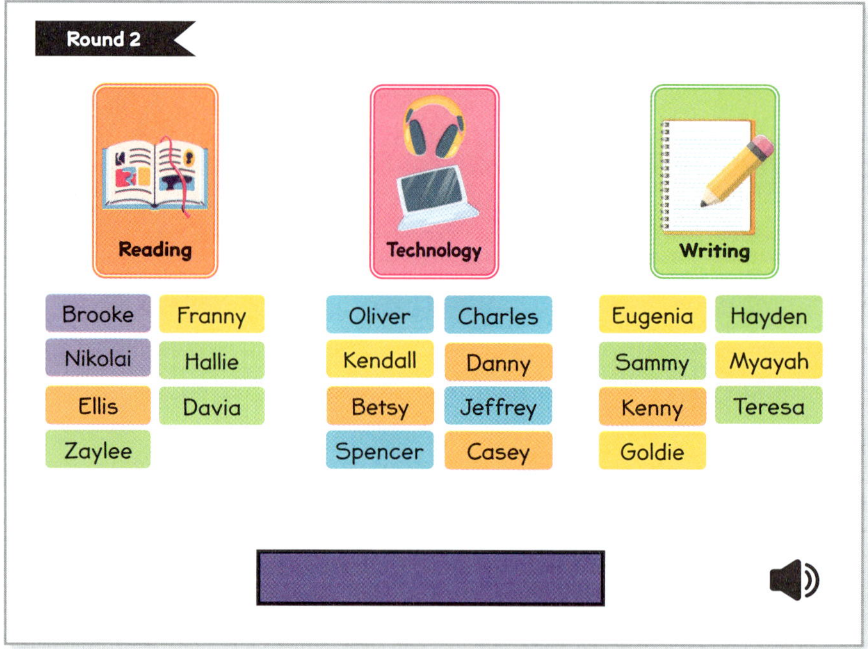

Rather than assigning a fixed icon on the PowerPoint with names for those working with me, I call over students to my reading table as needed. This helps me keep a more flexible and fluid grouping structure, since some groups need more time with me than others. While students may miss a portion of their current center, I strive to rotate the order of group pull-backs to ensure students get participation in each center throughout the week.

I don't give names to groups. Instead, I simply call back the students I need. But for the purpose of this chapter, let's assign numbers to the different groups:

Group 1: Alphabet Knowledge
Group 2: Decoding
Group 3: Decoding
Group 4: Fluency
Group 5: Vocabulary and Comprehension

BEHIND THE SCENES

Supporting Struggling Students

I try not to pull my most struggling readers from the technology center because the software program we use provides them with instruction in the phonics skills they need. I opt to pull them from the reading or writing center instead.

I prioritize the most vulnerable students. Students in Groups 1 and 2 meet with me every day, while others might meet with me 1–3 times a week. Here's what a daily schedule might look like:

Round 1	Round 2	Round 3
15 minutes	15 minutes	15 minutes
• I meet with **Group 3** for 9 minutes. • I meet with **Group 1** for 6 minutes.	• I continue to meet with **Group 1** for 9 minutes. • I have 1 minute to prep for **Group 2**. • I meet with **Group 2** for 5 minutes.	• I continue to meet with **Group 2** for 10 minutes. • I have 5 extra minutes to pull back a group of students to work on *b*'s/*d*'s.

The next day it might look like this:

Round 1	Round 2	Round 3
15 minutes	15 minutes	15 minutes
• I meet with **Group 3** for 10 minutes. • I meet with **Group 2** for 5 minutes.	• I continue to meet with **Group 2** for 7 minutes. • I have 1 minute to prep for **Group 1** • I meet with **Group 1** for 7 minutes.	• I continue to meet with **Group 1** for 6 minutes. • I meet with **Group 4** for 9 minutes.

TRANSITION TIP

Practice Rotating

We practice rotating to our new centers quickly and quietly. I often point out and praise students who have started their new center by the time the music's over.

✱ Kindergarten Note: I include the Explore Center every day in kindergarten. Our center time lasts 40–45 minutes with four core centers (reading, writing, technology, and explore). This breaks down to 10–11 minutes per center.

✱ First-Grade Note: I add the Explore Center on Fridays as a fun reward for students, bringing our center time to 60 minutes. This gives me time to work with a couple small groups and progress monitor students.

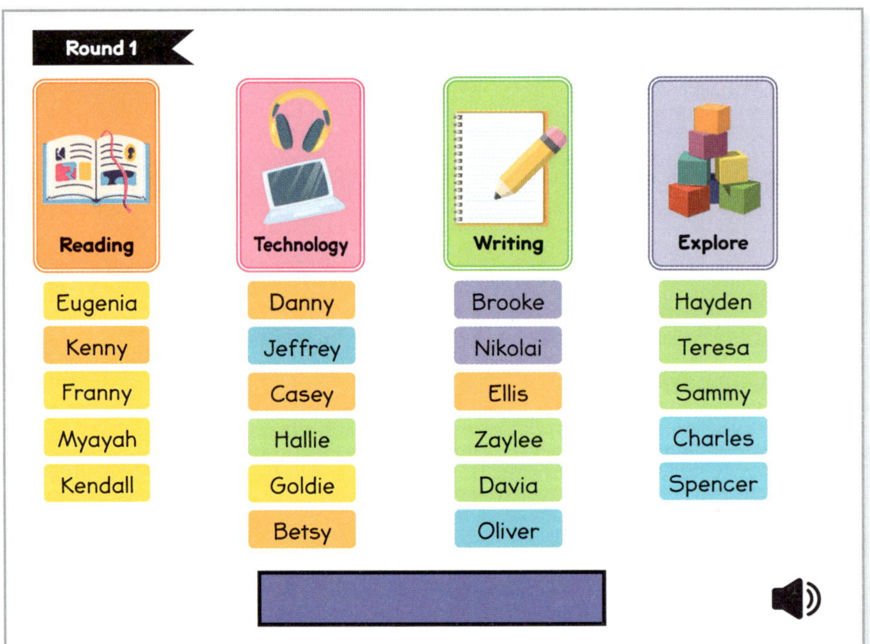

BEHIND THE SCENES Considering Student Needs

I carefully assign students to centers, making sure to separate any students that may work best apart from one another. These are mixed ability groupings. I offer special considerations when needed. For example, if centers come directly after our whole-class instruction, I might assign the Reading Center first to a student who needs a break and will benefit from listening to a read-aloud.

CENTERS VARIATION 2

In Variation 2, there are four 15-minute centers—Reading, Technology, Writing, and Word Work—with a parent volunteer running the Word Work Center.

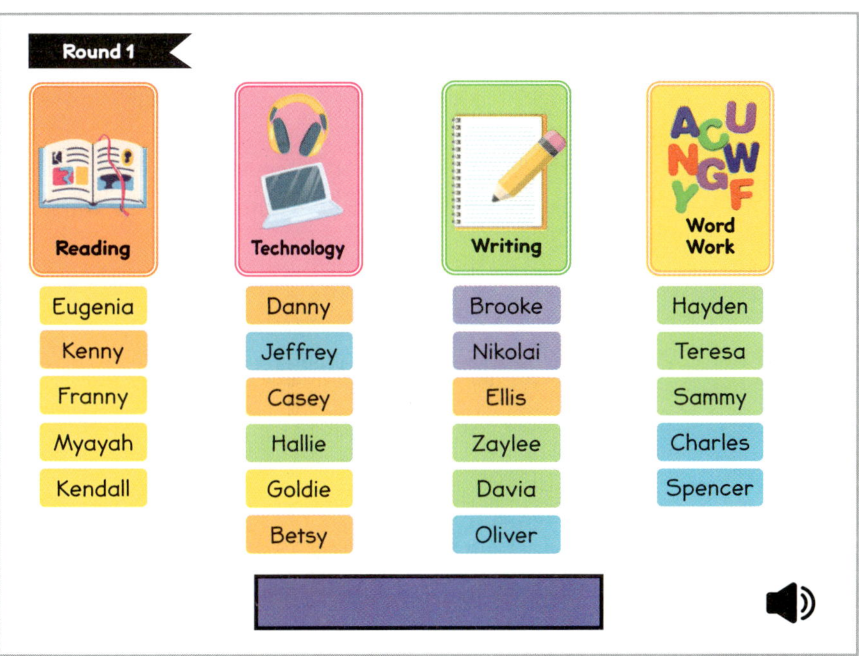

This gives me more time to work with small groups. I might extend each group's session by a few minutes, or I could keep the group minutes the same, and be able to meet with an additional group. So my small-group schedule might look something like this:

Rotation 1	Rotation 2	Rotation 3	Rotation 4
• I meet with **Group 4** or **Group 5** for 11 minutes. • I prep for 1 minute. • I meet with **Group 1** for 3 minutes.	• I continue to meet with **Group 1** for 15 minutes.	• I prep for 1 minute. • I meet with **Group 2** for 14 minutes.	• I prep for 1 minute. • I meet with **Group 3** for 12 minutes. • I have 2 minutes to prepare for the next activity or to monitor students.

Across the week, our schedule might look like this:

Monday	Tuesday	Wednesday	Thursday	Friday
Centers: 60 minutes (Variation 2) I meet with: Groups 1, 2, 3, 4.	**Centers: 45 minutes (Variation 1)** I meet with: Groups 1, 2, 3.	**Centers: 60 minutes (Variation 2)** Small-Group instruction: Groups 1, 2, 3, 5.	**Centers: 45 minutes (Variation 1)** I meet with: Groups 1, 2, 4.	**Centers: 60 minutes (Friday Variation 1)** I meet with Groups 1, 3, and progress monitor students.

Or if I keep student groups to 10–15 minutes, I can fit in more groups. My schedule might look like this:

Round 1	Round 2	Round 3	Round 4
• I meet with Group 4 for 10 minutes. • I meet with Group 1 for 5 minutes.	• I continue to meet with Group 1 for 10 minutes. • I meet with Group 2 for 5 minutes.	• I continue to meet with Group 2 for 10 minutes. • I meet with Group 3 for 5 minutes.	• I continue to meet with Group 3 for 5 minutes. • I meet with Group 5 for 10 minutes.

The plus side is that I've been able to meet with all my students. The downside is that I've met with some groups for only 10 minutes. My students' needs determine which way is more effective. Across the week, this schedule might look like this:

Monday	Tuesday	Wednesday	Thursday	Friday
Centers: 60 minutes I meet with Groups 1, 2, 3, 4, 5.	**Centers: 45 minutes** I meet with Groups 1, 2, 3.	**Centers: 60 minutes** I meet with: Groups 1, 2, 3, 4, 5.	**Centers: 45 minutes** I meet with: Groups 1, 2, 3.	**Centers: 60 minutes** I meet with Groups 1, 2, and progress monitor students.

First-grade teacher Virginia Quinn-Mooney says, "Whoever needs me the most, gets me the most." (2023). I agree. I make it a point to meet with my most struggling readers every single day. I meet with stronger readers twice a week. I progress monitor my students regularly to determine if my instruction and systems are working for them. If they are not, I can adjust my schedule to meet with these students more often or for longer.

Remember, when I devote more time for centers, I recruit a volunteer who can help students stay on task at their various centers. She can also troubleshoot technology or run a quick alphabet or high-frequency word review. Volunteers ensure that I have uninterrupted time as I work with small groups and also decrease the amount of time students are working independently.

> **✱ Kindergarten Note:** In Variation 2, I allot 10–12 minutes for each center (reading, writing, technology, explore, and word work) for 50–60 minutes total.

CENTERS VARIATION 3

The third variation might be the most effective of the three, but it's only possible if you have at least three adults available: the teacher and two volunteers. I like this variation because students get more instruction in small groups and less time at centers. This means they have more practice opportunities with feedback from a teacher. I dislike this variation because I don't get to work with all the students in my class. This is why I like to wait to start this option after I've had a few months to work with all students in small groups. At that time, I am more willing to release those who are progressing strongly to work with my aide or parent volunteer. I always keep the most needy students with me since I'm the most qualified. Students working independently rotate between two centers: technology and either reading or writing, alternating daily. The slides for this variation have fixed icons with me and my two assistants.

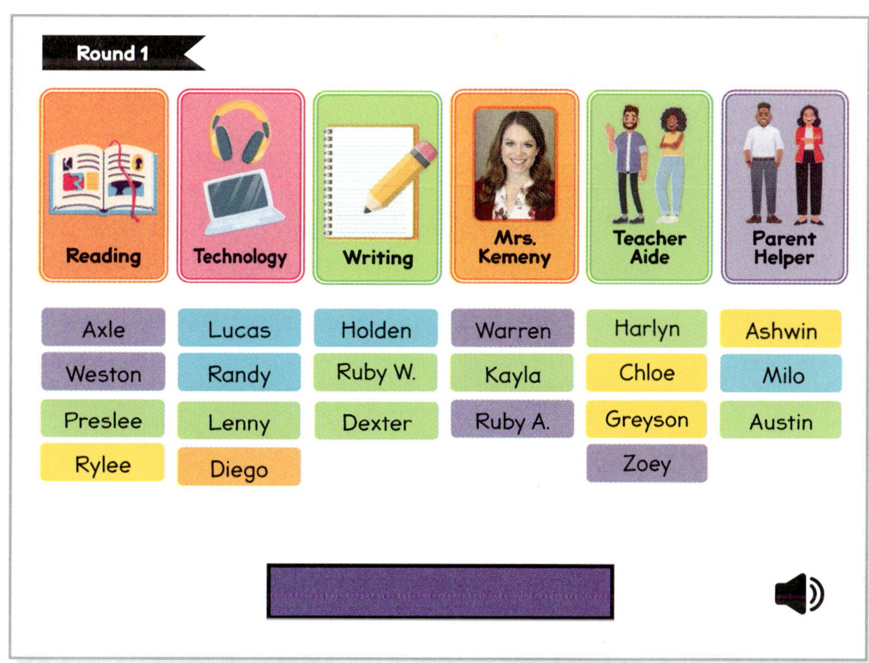

I meet with two groups for 30 minutes each, my aide works with a group for 30 minutes, and my parent volunteer works with two groups of my most advanced students for 30 minutes each. Other students are working at just two centers independently, for a total of 30 minutes of independent work for that day. I still have the PowerPoint slides rotate after 15 minutes so that the students working independently know when to switch to their second center. All the other students remain with their group when the slides switch.

The chart shows how this schedule might look.

Round 1	Round 2	Round 3	Round 4
15 minutes	15 minutes	15 minutes	15 minutes
• I meet with Group 1. • My aide works with Group 3. • My parent volunteer works with Group 4. • Students in Groups 2 and 5 work at either the technology or reading center independently.	• I continue to meet with Group 1. • My aide continues to work with Group 3. • My parent volunteer continues to work with Group 4. • Students in Groups 2 and 5 swap and work at either the technology or reading center independently.	• I meet with Group 2. • My parent volunteer works with Group 5. • Students in Groups 1, 3, and 4 work at the technology or reading center (with my aide assisting).	• I continue to meet with Group 2. • My parent volunteer continues to work with Group 5. • Students in Groups 1, 3, and 4 swap and work at either the technology or reading center independently.

Variation 3 is a great option because it gives us more time to complete all the elements of the small-group lesson described in this chapter. You might also shorten this time to just 30 minutes total for the day (rather than 60 minutes) and rotate stronger readers so they just meet in small groups twice a week or for less time. The table shows one way this might look.

Variation 3 (30 minutes total)

	Monday	Tuesday	Wednesday	Thursday
Teacher	Group 1	Group 1	Group 1	Group 1
Paraprofessional	Group 2	Group 2	Group 2	Group 2
Parent Volunteer	Group 3	Group 4 (15 minutes) Group 5 (15 minutes)	Group 3	Group 4 (15 minutes) Group 5 (15 minutes)
Independent Centers	Groups 4 and 5	Group 3	Groups 4 and 5	Group 3

If I have volunteers every day, I can use Variation 3 every day. If I only have them twice a week, my weekly schedule might look like this:

Monday: **Variation 3**
Tuesday: **Variation 1**
Wednesday: **Variation 3**
Thursday: **Variation 1**
Friday: **Friday Variation 1**

BEHIND THE SCENES

Reflecting on MTSS

In a multi-tiered system of support (MTSS), students who are struggling are provided with increasing levels of targeted support. These levels, or tiers, of support can look different from district to district. Most commonly, districts use three tiers of support. Tier 1 is what is provided for the whole class. This can include differentiated small groups. In Tiers 2 and 3, the support becomes more intense and individualized. If students are pulled out for a Tier 2/3 intervention during our center time, they work with the intervention teacher for 20–30 minutes and then I make sure they work with me for the next 15–30 minutes. They may not be able to work in centers at all, but that's okay because the instruction is so valuable.

Let's sum up these variations.

Variation 1: Students are in the three core centers (reading, writing, and technology) for 45 minutes (15 minutes each) while I pull three or four small groups. This variation works well if I am the only adult available during this time, but it's even better if I have an aide or volunteer who can assist the students working independently.

- **Kindergarten:** Students are in four core centers for 40 minutes (10 minutes each) while I pull around three or four small groups.
- **First Grade:** I add in the Explore Center on Friday. I either replace one of the core centers or add it in as a fourth center, if I have time for 60-minute centers.

Variation 2: Students are in four centers for 60 minutes (15 minutes each), while I pull four or five small groups. This variation works well if I have at least one other adult available to help during this time—it's even better if I have two. One volunteer helps students complete the Word Work Center and the other assists the other students working independently.

- **Kindergarten:** Students are in five core centers for 50–60 minutes (10–12 minutes each) while I pull four or five small groups.

Variation 3: Students are in two centers for 30 minutes (15 minutes each) and receive instruction in a small group for 30 minutes. This variation is only possible if there are three adults available during this time (the teacher and two volunteers).

Schedule Considerations: Finding Your Groove

How much time should you allot for centers? To ensure all students receive a strong foundation, explicit whole-class instruction is essential and should not be replaced by centers. Remember, my small-group instruction and center activities are a time to practice the skills we are learning in other parts of the day. So as I plan my literacy block, I prioritize core content, allocating remaining time for centers and small groups. If you only have 90 minutes for your literacy block, I'd recommend only spending 30 minutes for centers/small groups. If you have 120–150 minutes for your literacy block, you might be able to devote 45–60 minutes to centers/small groups. I wouldn't recommend going over 60 minutes. Be sure not to replace the whole-class instruction time. Because I find small-group time so beneficial, I love to dedicate an hour for centers when possible because it gives me more opportunities to work with students in small groups. However, I only do this when a parent volunteer or two can assist students, minimizing the time students are working independently.

There are so many ways to run centers and so many reasons to change and reevaluate them across the year. If I feel like my students' reading is taking off in the spring, and I'm able to meet students' needs in my whole-class instruction, I might shorten small group and centers time to only 30 minutes. Then I might use the additional time in our schedule to increase the time we have for writing instruction or to add in a fluency protocol called Partner Reading Paragraph Shrinking (see *7 Mighty Moves* page 123). The point is to be flexible, use your data, and do what is best for your students.

Your small groups and centers do not need to look exactly like mine. You may prefer to run four 10-minute centers each day. Or you may have enough volunteers to do Variation 3 for 30 minutes each day and have no need for center activities. Perhaps you have a "Must Do, May Do" system that works well for your students. That is all fine! I offer what I do simply as an example. The main thing is to make sure your students are engaged and on task in meaningful activities, allowing you to focus on the ones you've chosen for small groups.

In Closing, Remember...

Plan your small groups and centers! First, use assessment data to determine the needs of your students and divide them up into focused skill groups. From there, you need to determine how much time you have for centers in your classroom. Plan your whole-class instruction first to ensure you have time for explicit phonics, close reading, writing, math, and science/social studies.

Some questions to keep in mind include:

- How much time do you have left? 30 minutes? 45 minutes? 60 minutes?
- Do you have any other adults who can help you during this time?
- What center activities can students engage in?

Remember that center time is a time for students to practice skills they have already learned. Consider how you can make the most of your time and the resources available to you.

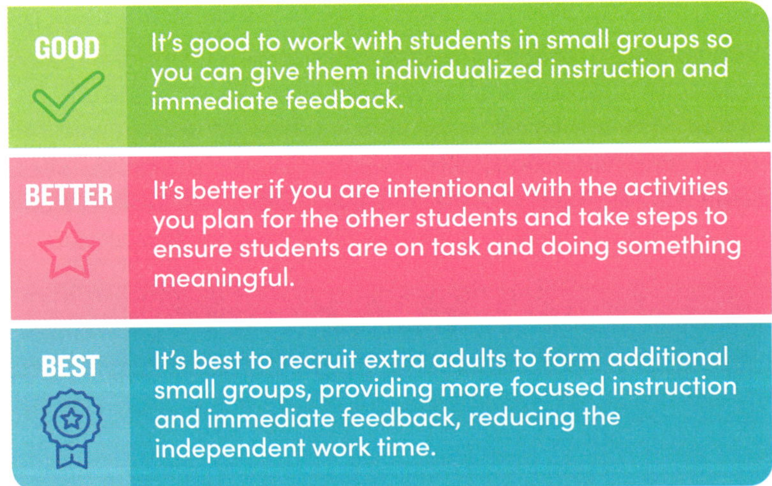

Encore! Read-Aloud

CHAPTER 7

SPOTLIGHT ON READ-ALOUDS

After a productive morning and energizing lunch, my students gather again on the rug for a delightful reading experience. Students settle in, ready to be transported by the story I'll be reading aloud. Sometimes the book I choose connects to our close-reading lesson, and sometimes it's simply a beautiful piece of literature I want to share. Regardless, read-aloud is a special time for all of us.

DOMINANT MOVE FROM *7 MIGHTY MOVES*

MOVE 7: Improve Comprehension by Developing Vocabulary and Background Knowledge

Do you have fond memories of someone reading to you? I do. I treasure the memories of my dad reading to me each night when I was little. I remember his powerful voice and expressions when he read classics, such as *The Little House* and *Mike Mulligan and His Steam Shovel*. I also remember the magic of listening to my teacher read *Tuck Everlasting* in elementary school.

Lindsay Live! Enter her classroom to learn more about read-alouds.

Fast forward to my student teaching days. I look back fondly at my mentor teacher's dramatic readings. She would put on a whole show, capturing each book's characters by varying her voice and acting out scenes as she read to her class after lunch. The students were captivated!

Fast forward even further to my own teaching. Last year, my daughter and her friend stopped by my classroom at lunch. I was immediately concerned when I saw they had been crying. When I asked what was wrong, they told me their teacher had just finished reading aloud *Where the Red Fern Grows*. I realized they had experienced a special moment; the read-aloud had touched them deeply.

A Closer Look at Read-Alouds

The purpose of reading aloud at this point in my literacy block is much different from the purpose of reading aloud during close-reading lessons. Here, it is for pure enjoyment! There's something really special about being gathered on the rug while I read a book to students. I love bonding with my students during this time, sharing heartwarming fiction and fascinating nonfiction. I love providing positive experiences with books, hoping it'll foster a deep appreciation for them and ignite a passion for reading. And there are other benefits to reading aloud.

- It builds oral-language skills and vocabulary because students are exposed to sophisticated language.
- It fosters empathy and understanding by exposing students to characters from diverse backgrounds and with unique challenges. Students learn to recognize and understand the feelings of others, promoting compassion.
- It enhances critical-thinking skills and builds background knowledge.

There's something really special about being gathered on the rug while I read a book to students.

Resist the urge to use prerecorded read-alouds, as tempting as that may be. It's much more engaging for students to listen to you read, plus it fosters connection and discussion. Learn to embrace the joy of reading to students and try to savor the moment!

In her wonderful book *Read Alouds for All Learners*, Molly Ness shares a study that found 50–70 percent of elementary teachers don't plan for their read-alouds (McCaffrey & Hisrich, 2017). Guilty! To be honest, I don't have the time or capacity to prepare for read-alouds because I spend so much time, before and after school, preparing for other lessons in the literacy block: phonics, close-reading, writing, and small groups. Not to mention planning for math, social studies, and science; emailing parents; reviewing student data; preparing materials; recruiting class volunteers; assembling supplies ready for that new student; morning duty; attending meetings; helping a team member; rearranging the seating chart; troubleshooting technology; and all the other things expected of a teacher!

So, yep, I'm totally guilty of not planning my read-alouds. And you know what? For now, I'm okay with that. I choose the books, set aside the time, read with expression, pause periodically to explain or question, and, after the reading, lead a discussion. Perhaps, in the future, I'll have the capacity to dedicate more time to plan, but for now I'm okay to settle in somewhere between what's "Good" and what's "Better" for this time of day.

But if you are ready to aim higher, Ness shares a three-step planning process (2023):

1. Evaluate: Read the text for vocabulary, background knowledge, and syntactical knowledge the author assumes the reader has. Identify any barriers to comprehension, such as vocabulary, gaps in knowledge, or complex sentence structure.
2. Explain: Think of ways to help students through the potential stumbling blocks you found in Step 1.
3. Engage and Extend: Consider opportunities for critical inquiry and reflection about the text. Ness advises considering social-emotional learning, cross-curricular extensions, and literacy extensions.

Amp Up Your Questions

I don't ask too many questions *during* the read-aloud because I don't want to interrupt the flow of the text. I tend to stop reading only to offer quick explanations of a word or concept. Sometimes, when I'm reading fiction, I have students make a prediction to get them further invested and excited about the story. I save the majority of the questions for after reading to spark conversation and help students understand and process the text. Admittedly, I am not great at coming up with questions on the spot, but I do my best. Here are some techniques that have helped me and, hopefully, can help as you create questions about the books you're reading.

Ask questions to help students determine the gist of the story. This is easy to fall back on because I do it regularly in my close-reading lessons. I ask, *Who is the main character?* Or *What is this book about?* Then I might ask, *What does the main character do?* Or *What is the author telling us about the topic?*

Ask questions to determine the text structure. Using the KAT framework (Wijekumar et al., 2023; see page 76), I can ask students questions to help them determine the text structure: comparison, cause and effect, or problem and solution. I can ask, *Was there a problem in the story? If so, what is it?* Then I might ask, *What caused the problem?* Then, *How was the problem solved?* From there, I can point out that the text has a problem-and-solution structure. If the problem is not solved, I might say, "This story had a problem, but not a solution. The problem is that the orangutans are struggling to find food and shelter, but the author didn't tell us how to fix this problem. What was the effect of this problem? Yes, the orangutan population is declining. This story has a cause-and-effect structure." This could lead into a discussion about what students think would be a good solution.

Ask questions to identify story elements. I use the acronym C-SPACE (see page 78) to teach my students story elements: character, setting, problem, actions, conclusion, and emotion. I might ask, *Who are the main characters? What is the Setting?*, etc.

TRANSITION TIP

Invite Partner Discussions

Before discussing questions as a whole class, I have students discuss them with an assigned partner to give everyone the opportunity to participate. To regain students' attention, I count backward "3-2-1-0." If students stop talking and are facing me by 0, they get a point on the T/S chart.

> **BEHIND THE SCENES**
> **Selecting Books**
> I love finding favorite books to read aloud to students. To stay up-to-date on the latest in children's literature, I rely on my school librarian for recommendations and websites, such as Maya's Book Nook, for diverse reading options.

Ask questions to help students understand the characters' actions or viewpoints. I might ask, *Why do you think the character did that?* Or *Why do you think the character feels that way?*

Ask questions to help connect the text to students' lives—such as, *What would you do if you were in this situation? Do you agree with what the character did? Why or why not?*

I also often ask, *What was your favorite part?*

My Favorite Books to Read Aloud

Do you need some ideas for read-aloud books? Here are some of my favorites.

***Alexander and the Wind-Up Mouse* by Leo Lionni** This is a sweet narrative of a little mouse who feels jealousy and envy toward another mouse, but ultimately demonstrates compassion when help is needed.

***The Dark* by Lemony Snicket** This book is scary, but not too scary! It's about a young boy who is afraid of the dark. The dark normally stays in the basement and leaves him alone, until one day...it doesn't. I read it in a spooky voice, and my students are completely transfixed.

***The Day the Crayons Quit* by Drew Daywalt** A young boy opens his crayon box to find a stack of letters addressed to him. Each letter is written by a different crayon, expressing its unique thoughts and feelings. Students love listening to this one over and over.

***The Dot* and *ish* by Peter H. Reynolds** I'm pairing these books because they share a similar message: the magic of believing in yourself. Both books beautifully illustrate how one person's confidence can inspire a chain reaction of positivity and hope.

***Each Kindness* by Jacqueline Woodson** Woodson delivers an important message about how a little kindness goes a long way. It's a serious story that doesn't end happily. My students aren't accustomed to hearing such stories, so their reactions are always interesting and lead to insightful discussions.

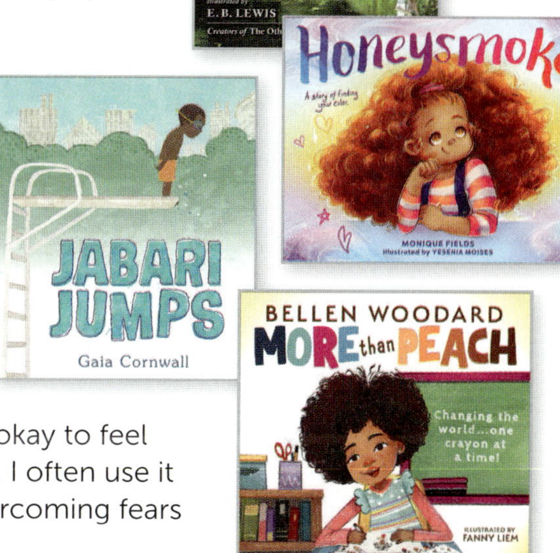

***The Empty Pot* by Demi** An emperor awards a seed to each child in the land, promising the kingdom to whoever can grow the most beautiful plant. Young Ping longs to be chosen, but his seed won't grow. What will he do? This is a beautiful story of integrity.

***Honeysmoke: A Story of Finding Your Color* by Monique Fields** I love this story of a young, biracial girl who looks around the world to find her color. It helps children see that people come in all colors, and that it's okay to take pride in your own beautiful and unique color.

***Jabari Jumps* by Gaia Cornwall** A young boy, Jabari, works up the courage to jump off the diving board, thanks to his dad's gentle reminder that it's okay to feel scared. This book teaches a valuable lesson. I often use it as a starting point for discussions about overcoming fears and taking safe risks.

More Than Peach* by Bellen Woodard** This story pairs nicely with ***Honeysmoke. It's the true story of a nine-year-old girl who is first confused and then troubled when her classmates call only the peach-colored crayon "skin colored." The girl sets out on a mission to expand the language we use to create safer, more inclusive spaces.

***Rocket Says Look Up!* by Nathan Bryon** Rocket is an aspiring astronaut who is passionate about space and the upcoming meteor shower. The problem is getting her brother and everyone else to look up from what they're doing. It's a charming book with beautiful pictures.

***Sideways Stories from Wayside School* by Louis Sachar** This book is so original, with an odd and hilarious event happening in each chapter. It always brings a lot of laughter into the classroom. It's best for second grade and up.

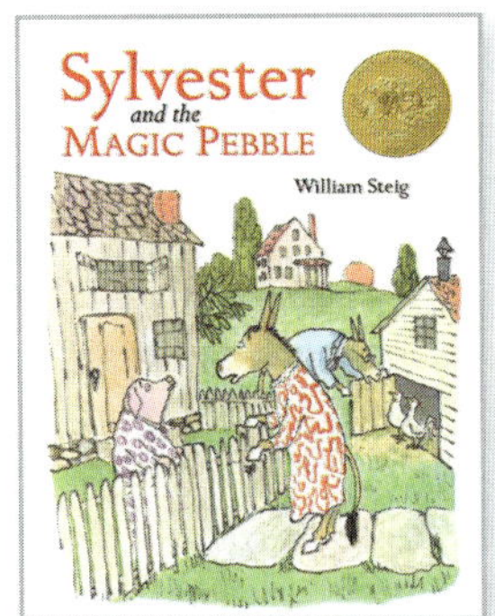

***Sylvester and the Magic Pebble* by William Steig**
This is another book that has captivated me since childhood. It's about a young donkey who finds a pebble that can grant any wish. When he hastily wishes to be a rock to escape a lion, the donkey finds himself in a precarious predicament. Students get so invested in this story and concerned whether Sylvester will ever join his family again.

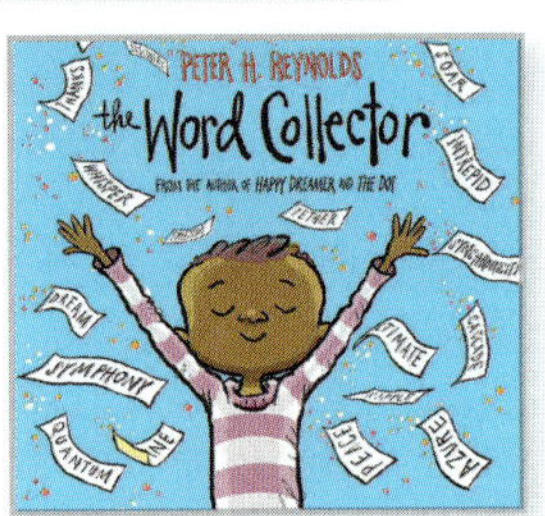

***Where the Sidewalk Ends* by Shel Silverstein**
Silverstein's lighthearted, witty poems have captivated me since childhood! It's a magical experience to share them with my students.

***The Word Collector* by Peter H. Reynolds**
As a literacy advocate, I adore this book about a young boy who loves to collect words. It's a great one to spark a conversation about the power of words and the ways we use them.

Schedule Considerations: Finding Your Groove

I usually spend anywhere between 10–20 minutes for this part of the day. The time of day and length of time I read aloud varies from year to year, depending on how my schedule works out. Sometimes it works best to read after lunch to give students a chance to settle down and prepare for more learning. Other years it works best to read at the very end of the day, before students go home. Regardless of the specific time, I make reading aloud a consistent part of my daily routine.

In Closing, Remember...

Reading aloud to students is a special part of the day. Cherish connecting and laughing with them. Besides providing a positive experience with books, reading aloud builds relationships, oral language, critical-thinking skills, knowledge about words and the world, and compassion. It's a memorable moment in your students' day and is sure to leave a lasting impression.

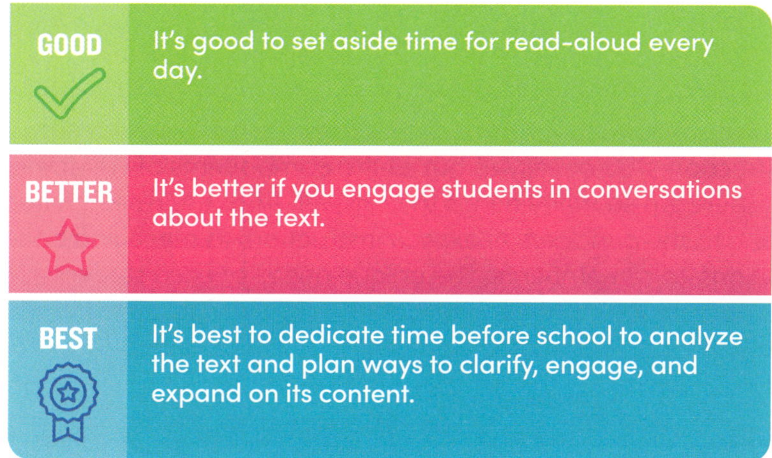

CONCLUSION

Ready to Rock?

There you have it: how I rock my literacy block! Now it's your turn. You get to figure out how to best organize your day and refine your instruction. It's not easy to put all the components of literacy instruction together. There are so many things to consider, from the research behind each component, to the principles of explicit instruction, to managing behaviors and transitions, to remembering the unique needs of each student. Certainly, it is a monumental task, but also a beautiful one. It's magical to witness children bloom into readers and writers. I hope reading about how I design my block inspires you as you design yours. Remember, there isn't one perfect way to structure your block. Perfection is not required. Take the ideas I share and make them your own. Adjust them to work for you and your students. Don't worry about perfection. Instead, focus on progression—both in your teaching and in your students' reading and writing. The decisions we make exist on a continuum from good to better to best. Do the best you can right now, knowing you'll continue to hone your instruction. Watch your class data to ensure what you're doing is working. If it's not, make some changes. Then share what's working with others so that, together, we can ensure that all students develop the literacy skills they need to succeed.

Are you ready to rock?

Let's review the essential points that will help you truly ROCK your literacy block.

R **Reflect** on your class data. Let the needs of your students guide your instruction and how you structure your day.

O **Optimize** your lessons by establishing consistent routines, a brisk instructional pace, and smooth classroom transitions.

C **Call** for frequent student responses to boost engagement and learning outcomes.

K **Keep** your focus on progress, not perfection—both in your teaching and in your students' reading and writing.

REFERENCES

Archer, A. (2022). Learning is not a spectator sport: Essentials of active participation. *Edview360 Blog Series*. https://www.voyagersopris.com/blog/edview360/learning-is-not-a-spectator-sport

Archer, A. L., & Hughes, C. A. (2010). *Explicit instruction: Effective and efficient teaching (What works for special-needs learners.)* Guilford Press.

Berninger, V. W., & Wolf, B. J. (2015). *Teaching students with dyslexia, dysgraphia, OWL LD, and dyscalculia (2nd ed.).* Brookes Publishing.

Birsh, J. R. (2018). *Multisensory teaching of basic language skills (1st ed.).* Brookes Publishing.

Cabell, S. Q., Justice, L. M., McGinty, A. S., DeCoster, J., & Forston, L. D. (2015). Teacher–child conversations in preschool classrooms: Contributions to children's vocabulary development. *Early Childhood Research Quarterly, 30*, 80–92.

Cardenas-Hagan, E. (2024). *Teachers of all things literacy, cultivating the genius in all children—language foundations for multiliteracy*. Big Sky Literacy Summit, Montana. https://www.thetransformativereadingteacher.com

Cook, C. R., Grady, E. A., Long, A. C., Renshaw, T., Codding, R. S., Fiat, A., & Larson, M. (2016). Evaluating the impact of increasing general education teachers' ratio of positive-to-negative interactions on students' classroom behavior. *Journal of Positive Behavior Interventions, 19*(2), 67–77.

Englert, C. S., Raphael, T. E., Anderson, L. M., Anthony, H. M., & Stevens, D. D. (1991). Making strategies and self-talk visible: Writing instruction in regular and special education classrooms. *American Educational Research Journal, 28*(2), 337–372.

Erbeli, F., Rice, M., Xu, Y., Bishop, M. E., & Goodrich, J. M. (2024). A meta-analysis on the optimal cumulative dosage of early phonemic awareness instruction. *Scientific Studies of Reading, 28*(4), 345–370.

Fuchs, D., Fuchs, L. S., Simmons, D., & Mathes, P. (2008). Peer assisted learning strategies: Reading methods for grades 2–6. Vanderbilt University.

Gough, P. B., & Tunmer, W. E. (1986). Decoding, reading, and reading disability. *Remedial and Special Education, 7*, 6–10.

Graham, S., Harris, K. R., McKeown, D. (2013) The writing of students with LD and a meta-analysis of SRSD writing intervention studies and future directions: Redux. In H. L. Swanson, K. R. Harris, & S. Graham (Eds), *Handbook of learning disabilities* (2nd ed., pp. 405–438). Guilford Press.

Hansford, N., Reenstra, E., & Laud, L. (2024). ThinkSRSD: A secondary analysis cohort investigation [Working Paper].

Harris, K. R. (2024). The self-regulated strategy development instructional model: Efficacious theoretical integration, scaling up, challenges, and future research. *Educational Psychology Review, 36*(4).

Harris, K. R., Graham, S., & Mason, L. (2003). Self-regulated strategy development in the classroom: Part of a balanced approach to writing instruction for students with disabilities. *Focus on Exceptional Children, 35*(7).

Harris, K. R., Kim, Y., Yim, S., Camping, A., & Graham, S. (2023). Yes, they can: Developing transcription skills and oral language in tandem with SRSD instruction on close reading of science text to write informative essays at grades 1 and 2. *Contemporary Educational Psychology, 73*, 102150.

Hudson, A. K., Owens, J. K., Moore, K. A., Lambright, K., & Wijekumar, K. (2021). What's the main idea? Using text structure as a framework for accelerating strategic comprehension of text. *Reading Teacher, 75*(1), 113.

Jennings, T. M., & Haynes, C. W. (2018). *From talking to writing: Strategies for scaffolding narrative and expository writing*. Landmark School Outreach Program.

Kemeny, L. (2023). *7 mighty moves: Research-backed, classroom-tested strategies to ensure K–3 reading success*. Scholastic.

Kemeny, L. (2025). *7 mighty moves reading resources: Ready-to-use tools and templates to transform your teaching*. Scholastic.

Kim, Y. S. G., Harris, K. R., Goldstone, R., Camping, A., & Graham, S. (2024). The science of teaching reading is incomplete without the science of writing: A randomized control trial of integrated teaching of reading and writing. *Scientific Studies of Reading*, 32–54.

Klingerman, J. (2024, April 1). The Reading League PA: Maximizing Your Literacy Block with Dr. Julie Klingerman [Video]. YouTube. https://www.youtube.com/watch?v=_funUZ3glMY

Klingner, J., Vaughn, S., & Schumm, J. (1998). Collaborative strategic reading during social studies in heterogeneous fourth-grade classrooms. *Elementary School Journal, 99*(1).

Laud, L., & Patel, P. (2023). *Releasing writers: Bring the science of writing & self-regulated strategy development (SRSD) alive in your classroom*. thinkAUM.

MacArthur, C. A., Schwartz, S. S., & Graham, S. (1991). A model for writing instruction: Integrating word processing and strategy instruction into a process approach to writing. *Learning Disabilities Research & Practice, 6*(4), 230–236.

MacSuga-Gage, A. S., & Simonsen, B. (2015). Examining the effects of teacher-directed opportunities to respond on student outcomes: A systematic review of the literature. *Education and Treatment of Children, 38*(2), 211–239.

Mason, L. H., Reid, R., & Hagaman, J. L. (2012). *Building comprehension in adolescents*. Brookes Publishing

McCaffrey, M., & Hisrich, K. E. (2017). Read-alouds in the classroom: A pilot study of teachers' self-reporting practices. *Reading Improvement, 54*(3), 93–100.

Moats, L., C. & Foorman, B. R. (2008). Literacy achievement in the primary grades in high-poverty schools. In S. Neuman (Ed.), *Educating the other America: Top experts tackle poverty, literacy, and achievement in our schools* (pp. 91–111). Brookes Publishing.

Moats, L. C., & Tolman, C. (2024). *Language essentials for teachers of reading and spelling (LETRS) Units 5–8* (3rd ed., Vol. 2). Voyager Sopris Learning.

National Reading Panel (2000). Teaching children to read: An evidence-based assessment of the scientific research literature on reading and its implications for reading instruction. National Institute of Child Health and Human Development.

Ness, M., & Kenny, M. (2016). Improving the quality of think-alouds. *The Reading Teacher 69*(4), 453–460.

Ness, M. (2023). *Read alouds for all learners: A comprehensive plan for every subject, every day, grades PreK–8*. Solution Tree Press.

Puzio, K., Colby, G. T., & Algeo-Nichols, D. (2020). Differentiated literacy instruction: Boondoggle or best practice? *Review of Educational Research, 90*(4), 459–498.

Quinn-Mooney, V. (2023, August 28). What structured literacy looks like in first grade (episode 132). https://podcasts.apple.com/us/podcast/what-structured-literacy-looks-like-in-first-grade/id1498200908?i=1000625895567

Reading Horizons. (2019). *Reading horizons discovery teacher's manual*, Chapter 1 (7th ed.).

Roberts, T. A., Vadasy, P. F., & Sanders, E. A. (2019). Preschoolers' alphabet learning: Cognitive, teaching sequence, and English proficiency influences. *Reading Research Quarterly, 54*(3), 413–437

Scarborough, H. S. (2001). Connecting early language and literacy to later reading (dis)abilities: Evidence, theory, and practice. In S. Neuman & D. Dickinson (Eds.), *Handbook of early literacy research, Volume 1* (pp. 97–110). Guilford Press.

Shanahan, T. (2019, January 26). How would you schedule the reading instruction? Shanahan on Literacy. https://www.shanahanonliteracy.com/blog/how-would-you-schedule-the-reading-instruction

Shanahan, T. (2005). The National Reading Panel Report. Practical Advice for Teachers. Learning Point Associates/North Central Regional Educational Laboratory (NCREL).

Simmons, K., Carpenter, L., Crenshaw, S., & Hinton, V. M. (2015). Exploration of classroom seating arrangement and student behavior in a second-grade classroom. *Georgia Educational Researcher 12*(1).

Smith, J. B., Lee, V. E., & Newmann, F. M. (2001). Instruction and achievement in Chicago elementary schools. UCHICAGO Consortium on School Research.

Stevens, E., & Austin, C. (2022). Structured reading comprehension intervention for students with reading difficulties. In L. Spear-Swerling (Ed.), *Structured literacy interventions* (pp. 165–167). Guilford Press.

Sutherland, K. S., Wehby, J. H., & Copeland, S. R. (2000). Effect of varying rates of behavior-specific praise on the on-task behavior of students with EBD. *Journal of Emotional and Behavioral Disorders, 8*(1), 2–8.

Tobia, V., Sacchi, S., Cerina, V., Manca, S., & Fornara, F. (2020). The influence of classroom seating arrangement on children's cognitive processes in primary school: The role of individual variables. *Current Psychology, 41*(9), 6522–6533.

Underwood, S. (2018). What is the evidence for an uninterrupted, 90-minute literacy instruction block? Education Northwest. http://educationnorthwest.org/resources/what-evidenceuninterrupted-90-minute-literacyinstruction-block

Vaughn, S., Swanson, E. A., Roberts, G., Wanzek, J., Stillman-Spisak, S. J., Solis, M., & Simmons, D. (2013). Improving reading comprehension and social studies knowledge in middle school. *Reading Research Quarterly, 48*(1), 77–93.

West, T. (2017, April 25). All about centers! (A freebie guide!). Little Minds at Work. https://littlemindsatwork.org/centers-freebie-guide/

Wijekumar, K., Hudson, A., Lambright, K., Owens, J. K., Binks-Cantrell, E., Beerwinkle, A., & Stack, A. (May/June, 2023). Knowledge acquisition and transformation (KAT) using text structures. *The Reading League Journal, 4*(2), 33–39.

Wlodkowski, R. J. (1983). Motivational opportunities for successful teaching [Leader's Guide]. Universal Dimensions.

Woolf, N. (2024, March 18). 2x10 relationship building: How to do it (and why it works!). Panorama Education. https://www.panoramaed.com/blog/2x10-relationship-building-strategy

Zucker, T. A., & Cabell, S. Q. (2023). *Strive-for-five conversations: A framework that gets kids talking to accelerate their language comprehension and literacy*. Scholastic.

INDEX

K

L

M

N

O

P

Q

R

S